The
Empowered
Professor

The Empowered Professor

Breaking the Unspoken Codes of Inequity in Academia

Dana Mitra

TEACHERS COLLEGE PRESS

TEACHERS COLLEGE | COLUMBIA UNIVERSITY
NEW YORK AND LONDON

Published by Teachers College Press,® 1234 Amsterdam Avenue, New York, NY 10027

Library of Congress Cataloging-in-Publication Data

Names: Mitra, Dana L., author.
Title: The empowered professor : breaking the unspoken codes of inequity
    in academia / Dana Mitra.
Description: New York, N.Y. : Teachers College Press, [2022] | Includes
    bibliographical references and index.
Identifiers: LCCN 2021025780 (print) | LCCN 2021025781 (ebook) |
    ISBN 9780807766293 (paperback) | ISBN 9780807766309 (hardcover) |
    ISBN 9780807780701 (ebook)
Subjects: LCSH: College teaching—United States. | College teachers—
    United States. | Mentoring in education—United States.
Classification: LCC LB2331 .M498 2022 (print) | LCC LB2331 (ebook) |
    DDC 378.1/250973—dc23
LC record available at https://lccn.loc.gov/2021025780
LC ebook record available at https://lccn.loc.gov/2021025781ISBN

ISBN 978-0-8077-6629-3 (paper)
ISBN 978-0-8077-6630-5 (hardcover)
ISBN 978-0-8077-8070-1 (ebook)

Printed on acid-free paper
Manufactured in the United States of America

*In memory of Suet-ling Pong, who taught me the unspoken
rules at Penn State and modeled what a mentor can be.*

Contents

Acknowledgments   xi

1. **Introducing a Coaching Approach to Faculty Development**   1

    Faculty Can Find Agency and Purpose   2

    Universities Can Bolster Faculty Development   2

    Framework: The Intersection of Structure and Agency as a
        Pathway to Fulfillment   3

    Part I: Breaking the Institutional Code   4

    Part II: Strengthening Academic Identity   5

    PART I: BREAKING THE INSTITUTIONAL CODE

2. **Unspoken Structures in the Academic Code**   11

    Identifying Codified Structures   12

    Normative Processes—The Culture   13

    Cognitive Processes: Hidden Beliefs and Structures   15

    Implicit Bias and Privilege as Cognitive Structures   15

    Creating an Inclusive and Welcoming Climate   17

    Addressing Grievances   19

    The Institution of Tenure   20

    Recommendations for Universities   23

3. **The Inner Critic**   24

    Shame Triggers With the Inner Critic   25

    Finding the Inner Critic in the Body   26

Stepping Away From the Inner Critic   27

Rumination: The Inner Critic on Repeat   28

Inner Critics and Stress Response   30

Getting Unstuck From Writer's Block   31

The Critic in Academia: Peer Review   32

Speak Your Truth   34

Recommendations for Universities   35

PART II: STRENGTHENING ACADEMIC IDENTITY

4. **Agency**   **39**

Tapping Into a Deeper Purpose   39

Charge Batteries; Don't Drain Them   40

Learning What Purpose Feels Like   41

Identifying Core Values   42

Purpose as Career-Long Trajectory   42

Finding Leaders and Mentors Within   44

Recommendations for Universities   48

5. **Research**   **49**

Building a Scholarly Identity   49

Maximizing Publishing While Protecting Purpose   51

When Purpose Questions Dominant Paradigms   53

Recommendations for Universities   55

6. **Belonging**   **56**

Connecting to Others   57

Intellectual Spaces: Finding Collaborators   58

Multiple Sources of Support   59

Building a Community   60

Collaborations Gone Awry   61

    Strategic Conferencing   62

    Network Everywhere   65

    Identifying Cultural Biases Related to Communication   66

    Support Spaces: How to Find Mentors   68

    Outside Letter Writers   70

    Finding Belonging Within and Beyond Academia   71

    Recommendations for Universities   72

7. Service   73

    Chosen Service—"Want-to-Do" Work   73

    Required Service—"Must-Do" Work   75

    Service That Can Be Avoided—The Art of Saying No   77

    Mid-Career Academics: Creatively Broadening Contribution   79

    Recommendations for Universities   81

8. Competencies   82

    Goal-Setting   83

    Time Management: "Plan Your Work, Work Your Plan"   86

    Identifying Self-Care   88

    Delete, Delay, Delegate, Diminish   90

    Productivity   92

    Recommendations for Universities   96

9. Teaching   97

    Getting Rid of Inner Critics in the Classroom   97

    Improved Confidence in the Classroom   97

    Overcoming Imposter Syndrome   98

    Competencies of Teaching   99

    Competencies of Online Teaching   101

    Competencies of Simplified Grading   102

    Addressing Structures That Replicate Bias and Discrimination   103

Empowering Students by Creating Equitable Classroom Spaces   105

Recommendations for Universities   108

10. Conclusion   109

Appendix A: List of Core Values   111

Appendix B: My Strategic Plan, 2017–2018   115

Appendix C: Sample Paper Rubric   119

References   121

Index   135

About the Author   145

Acknowledgments

I wrote this book to bridge the two parts of my work identity—my professor self and my coach self. It felt risky to do so—to blend worlds that work on different sets of norms and frameworks. Pulling them together helped me to show the ways in which they feel drawn from the same sense of purpose within me—paving the way for others to amplify their voices in schools and universities.

Thank you to Brian Ellerbeck at Teachers College Press for taking a chance on this hybrid scholarship and being the type of editor we all hope to have. Thank you also to Karl Nyberg, my production editor, for your patience and thoughtful care of shepherding my manuscript to the finishing line.

Thank you to my colleagues who took the time to read drafts and provide invaluable feedback, literature, and encouragement, including Kevin Kinser, Kimberly Griffin, and Royel Johnson. Former students provided my first practice in coaching and serve as an inspiration as their careers bloom, including Kristina Brezicha, Catharine Biddle, Daniella Hall, Emily Hodge, and Emily Anderson. Gratitude to Karen Seashore and Megan Tschannen-Moran for modeling "Professors Who Coach" and being fellow travelers in this hybrid work. Thank you to Stephanie Knight and Gaetann Jean-Marie for your support of the book.

I am grateful to be invited to engage in the higher education consulting community of practice—colleagues who work as coaches in higher education settings. They created a safe space to birth the idea of this book and have been champions throughout the process. Thank you especially to Rena Seltzer and Diana Kardia for modeling encouragement and collegiality, and for showing me how we can lift each other up as we travel similar paths.

My understanding of how coaching can support academics began with my own need to seek coaching while balancing a pre-tenure job and two children in diapers. Stephanie Yost guided my path more than once and gave me permission to feel all the feelings and to provide agency to my process. Namaste. My own decision to become a certified coach arose through being called by others to ask me to help them through struggles at work, in relationships, and within themselves. My training with the CTI—the Coaches Training Institute—proved to be an all-in experience where I learned as much about myself as about how to support others. My path would not be the same without the instructors and fellow classmates I met along this journey. It was through this process that I felt ready to hang out my own shingle and to begin my own work as a coach focused on leadership, writing, and academic pathways. I learned through this training that my coaching focus is on helping others to define their purpose, to maintain balance, and to find pathways to productivity.

My own network of support will always include Stephanie Serriere. Thank you for being my first work partner and forever a sister. Weekly walks with Katherine Genovese affirmed my intentions and provided me with wise counsel and deep wisdom. Michele Dimidio provided unconditional love and laughter. Carolyn Hutter creates a safe place to tell it true in all its messiness, to fall apart and and pick myself back up again. Heidi Lewis and BJ Weaver both showed up in my first coaching workshop and continue with me as fellow travelers, learning how to live our best versions of ourselves and keeping one another honest along the way.

My husband, Todd, and my mom and dad remain my forever cheerleaders and support network as I work through drafts and juggle my own balancing act of parenting, daughtering, and marriage. Kaden and Carson (my human kiddos) are the reason for the journey. Kodiak, Tenzi, and Mountain (the menagerie) offer laughter and emotional support along the way.

The
Empowered
Professor

CHAPTER 1

Introducing a Coaching Approach to Faculty Development

Becoming an academic does not have the same romantic vision of an ivory tower that it might once have had. Stories abound of the shrinking of resources: of the replacement of tenure-track positions with increased part-time instructors; of the shrinking of grant opportunities; of faculty increasingly paying out-of-pocket for work expenses, including travel. This lack of resources is coupled with student stressors of increased mental distress, helicopter parents, and declining financial aid.

Beyond these new problems, universities still do not reflect the ever-increasing diversity of our society. Instead, the culture of academia remains predominantly White, male, heterosexual, cisgender, and able-bodied. Succeeding in academia involves mastering a culture that was originally designed for White men. It is a process of navigating unspoken rules, many of which contain explicit biases, while maintaining one's own sense of purpose and integrity. Universities have an obligation to improve transparency of structures and commit to a focus on increasing equity. Faculty members also must commit to engaging in the work of understanding the supports and struggles of university structures, and they also must commit to understanding themselves.

I wrote this book after spending over a decade coaching academics on how to find success and fulfillment in their careers. Faculty came to me when they had been knocked to the ground and found insufficient support institutionally. Some had their publications caught in a spin cycle of endless revisions; others had negative teaching reviews in successive semesters. Still others had negative supervisor feedback but not precise enough to indicate how to do any better. These struggles turned into self-doubt when faculty internalized criticism and viewed it to be reflective of their self-worth. They began to wonder if they really belonged in the academy.

The book speaks to two audiences: people working in academic jobs and university officials. In speaking to both, it walks the line of learning how faculty can try to succeed within a system while articulating the range of reforms needed so that universities can support and retain quality faculty.

FACULTY CAN FIND AGENCY AND PURPOSE

For faculty, and graduate students hoping to become faculty, this book offers advice and strategies based on research, looking at the nexus of human development and institutions—the space in which faculty can find success in universities. It emphasizes the skills needed to be a successful academic, with a focus on lifespan learning, including mid-career needs. It will benefit faculty at a range of universities and colleges, as well as graduate students considering academic careers and research scientists.

This book can also be useful for academics facing the job market. It can help to identify how to learn more about the universities one is considering, and it can also help candidates to better understand themselves as academics, including how to articulate one's purpose. This articulation can help one to discern their own fit with possible positions and also help academics define themselves and their work more clearly to others.

Mid-career faculty seeking guidance are often filled with restlessness and a shift of purpose. They may have overcome cultural barriers and succeeded—checked all the boxes, earned the gold stars, and achieved their tenure and promotion goals. Yet after all of that, they find themselves wondering if they have lost their own core sense of purpose in the process. They seek a renewed connection to the values, ethics, and curiosity that brought them to academia. They long to find a more fulfilled way to engage with their work.

UNIVERSITIES CAN BOLSTER FACULTY DEVELOPMENT

For universities, this book articulates how institutions can implement an equity-driven plan for faculty development. Although most universities provide a similar statement of intending to create equitable spaces, few schools have a thorough and consistent faculty development strategy that is inclusive and supportive for a diverse faculty (Gillespie & Robertson, 2010; Hansman & McAtee, 2014), including creating an expectation that equity is a responsibility of all faculty, especially those with the greatest power and privilege.

Recruiting and retaining a diverse faculty requires a focus not just on hiring, but on retention. Institutions have a responsibility to identify ways to address equity by providing proactive support to underrepresented faculty members—defined in this book to include faculty of color, women, LGBTQ people, first-generation college attenders, international faculty, and others for whom the culture and structure of academia is culturally and structured at odds with one's own identities and cultures.

The benefits of faculty development across the lifespan of a career are well-documented. Investments in faculty development have been shown to lead to robust improvements in research innovation, faculty quality of life, and discussion and dialogue across disciplines (Barlett & Rappaport, 2009; Blackburn & Lawrence, 1995; Gappa, Austin, & Trice, 2007; Hagedorn, 2000; O'Meara, Terosky, & Neumann, 2008). Faculty development also has been found to improve the retention and satisfaction of faculty, as well as commitment to the organization (O'Meara & Terosky, 2010).

Traditional faculty development usually takes a university-centered approach. It tends to focus on one-size-fits-all, large-group structures such as webinars and workshops (Haras, 2018). These opportunities also tend to focus primarily on improving academic teaching (e.g., Pallas & Neumann, 2019) or learning about a research area (Gonzales & Rincones, 2012; Lattuca, 2001; Neumann, 2009; O'Meara, Rivera, Kuvaeva, & Corrigan, 2017). Support for diverse faculty often is being outsourced in universities, such as offering funding for online programs on improving writing productivity and offering a cohort model of support.

This book instead argues that the true pathway to achieving greater retention of a diverse and inclusive faculty must focus on increasing support strategies that are designed with a coaching stance in mind. Research shows consistent evidence of the benefits of coaching for career persistence and retention in academic careers (Grover & Furnham, 2016; Lochmiller, 2014; Rhodes & Fletcher, 2013; Silver, Lochmiller, Copland, & Tripps, 2009; Williams, Thakore, & McGee, 2016a, 2016b). Such a strategy focuses on the individual needs of faculty, not just on their research topic or how to teach undergraduates, but an ongoing examination of themselves as learners (Neumann 2009) and an ability to embrace people as representing a broad range of intersectional identities (Crenshaw, 2017). A coaching stance meets the needs of faculty where they are and helps them to make progress in their work, including tailoring supports to specific university cultures as well as creating a space for encouraging cohort coaching in order to provide support across faculty.

FRAMEWORK: THE INTERSECTION OF STRUCTURE AND AGENCY AS A PATHWAY TO FULFILLMENT

This book examines the space in which individuals can find success within institutional settings while maintaining their own integrity. Many books looking at faculty improvement have been critiqued as "fix the struggling" (Hogan, 2010; Pyke, 2015). Rather than accepting the problematic viewpoint that individuals must change themselves to adjust to a biased system, this book instead offers an equity-driven model of faculty development.

This book draws on the growing scholarship demonstrating that university structures are embedded with inequity and bias favoring the privileged (Crenshaw, 2017; Delgado & Stefanic, 2017; Ladson-Billings & Tate,

1995; O'Meara & Terosky, 2010). It examines how faculty development must address the biased social-cultural contexts of universities while providing space to enable the individual agency possible within these contexts. The onus for creating equitable spaces must be on the university, and yet the book also recognizes that as the process continues, faculty must endure the burden of learning how to master structures that unfairly place heavier burdens on some faculty than they do on others.

The book builds out of a tradition of work looking at finding the nexus between structure and agency (Barley & Tolbert, 1997; Blackburn & Lawrence, 1995; Giddens, 1984). The chapters in this book draw on research from sociology and organizational theory to identify institutional structures that must be interrogated, and from human development, psychology, and coaching theory, to consider ways that individual faculty capacity can be strengthened through a stronger academic identity.

PART I: BREAKING THE INSTITUTIONAL CODE

To understand—and to challenge—the unspoken rules of the academy, faculty development should include an awareness of how an individual can understand and make choices on how to engage with sociocultural, institutional, and political contexts (Blackburn & Lawrence, 1995; O'Meara & Terosky, 2010). When important realities are implicit, they can prevent those without privilege and insider knowledge from finding success in a system. Embedded assumptions lead to inequities (Drago & Colbeck, 2003; Colbeck & Wharton-Michael, 2006).

Part I of this book explores the institutional rules of success embedded in academic jargon, cultural norms, and taken-for-granted behaviors. It begins by examining ways to investigate how the structures contribute to inequities, and it shows how to shine a light on the unspoken assumptions and lack of clarity of institutional processes.

Chapter 2 explores institutional rules, embedded rituals, and unspoken norms. It considers ways in which universities can commit to equity by attending to this unspoken code, and it also discusses the ways faculty can investigate and interrogate their organizational cultures. The chapter begins with the processes of systematically collecting data that identify the rules in the institution and then considers processes for how to make strategic choices about when to refute the system and when to consciously choose to work within the system. Included in this exploration is a focus on how conflict can and cannot be expressed, on the pathways for receiving support—formally and informally—and on understanding how grievances might be addressed if they arise.

Chapter 3 looks at how individuals can internalize bias as individual fault. By connecting institutional theory with concepts in coaching frameworks, the chapter describes how individuals take in biased, negative messaging as truth. The chapter explores how identification of inner critics can facilitate a better separation between oneself and these damaging messages.

PART II: STRENGTHENING ACADEMIC IDENTITY

Part II examines the building blocks needed for faculty success. Rather than teaching how to fit into institutions, this part of the book focuses on learning how to acquire the scaffolding needed to feel supported and strong. It examines the spaces in which individuals can find success within institutional settings while maintaining their own integrity, and it focuses on how to keep one's values and purpose clear. It includes finding communities of support and information, and developing a set of habits and skills that can sharpen one's focus on what matters.

Part II introduces processes needed for the development of one's academic identity—Agency, Belonging, and Competencies. The ABC Framework is derived from empirical research examining the developmental processes of becoming a change agent (Mitra, 2004; Mitra & Serriere, 2012). This framework serves as the foundation for achieving well-being and fulfillment as a faculty member. It aligns and is supported by research looking at motivation and academic/career success (Eccles & Gootman, 2002; Eccles, Midgley, Wigfield, Buchanan, Reuman, Flanagan, & MacIver, 1993; Roeser, Midgley, & Urdan, 1996) and faculty development research (Stupnisky, BrckaLorenz, Yuhas, & Guay, 2018). I intertwine these identity-building blocks with the core components of an academic career—research, teaching, and service. Figure 1.1 shows this relationship.

It must be stressed that although this part of the book focuses on faculty needs, the onus should be on institutions to provide support for this work; it is not the job of faculty members alone. More equitable and transparent structures can increase the support of faculty along the tenets of ABC developmental needs. The "Recommendations for Universities" boxes at the end of each of these chapters focus on the ways that universities can increase responsibility for these aspects of faculty development.

Chapter 4, "Agency," explores how to embody a confident and brave academic persona linked to purpose. This chapter is the foundation of the remainder of the book, with the Belonging and Competencies processes building on this foundation. Agency in a developmental context refers to the ability to "[act or exert] influence and power in a given situation" (Mitra, 2004, p. 655).

In higher education, agency includes a relationship to "thought" over time (Elder, 1997; O'Meara & Terosky, 2010)—that is, how faculty conceive of their "work" in relation to all of their identities and roles. This sense of identity is intertwined with the ability to exert power within the

Figure 1.1. Academic Structures and the ABC Framework

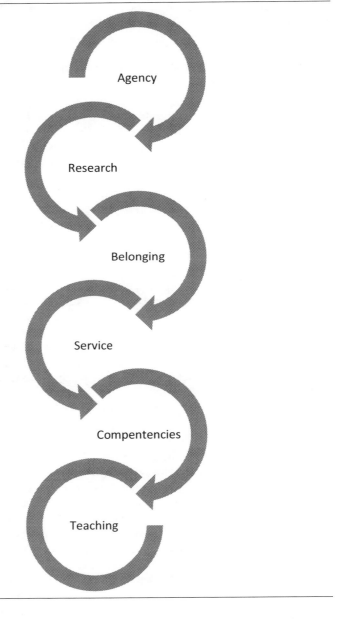

institutions in which faculty work. Agency is always constructed within a social and political context. Faculty need tools and strategies to identify core values and to draw from positive archetypes to develop a clear research agenda.

Chapter 5, "Research," explores how having a clear sense of agency can help create a clear and narrow research agenda by connecting to a broader purpose. Making voice clear and strong, emphasizing contribution, and communicating the value of one's work are introduced as key strategies for success. Faculty must build their brands as much as other careers, through research emphasis, presentations, and publications and by becoming memorable to colleagues. Chapter 5 looks at mid-career slumps and considers creative ways to find new purpose in one's roles and work.

"Belonging" (Chapter 6) explores how to strengthen agency by collaborating with others and connecting to communities. Breaking the academic code while still completing the day-to-day work of an academic is an exhausting prospect. Drawing on the research of communities of practice, this chapter shows how finding community can boost research productivity and improve work/life balance. It considers the range of communities needed, including peer learning communities, affinity groups, and research collaborators. It also identifies five kinds of mentors—confidants, political insiders, connectors, sponsors, and coaches.

"Service" (Chapter 7) connects belonging to learning how to engage in a profession in ways that deepen purpose and align with one's values. It introduces a model of discernment for choosing service based on work one wants to do, has to do, or can refuse, and considers the unspoken rules of how to maximize political visibility of service while finding ways to deflect service that would take large amounts of time away from writing and research.

"Competencies" (Chapter 8) considers the skills and abilities needed to build agency as an academic. It identifies goal-setting and time management as especially critical for faculty success, and it considers the unspoken guidelines for how to control workload and subsequently reduce stress.

Finally, "Teaching" (Chapter 9) shows how to model the work of breaking the code of academia for students. It considers how to make content and processes more transparent in teaching, while also making teaching more fulfilling by connecting it more closely to purpose. Chapter 9 examines structural biases that affect underrepresented faculty in teaching settings, and it also covers ways to improve teaching skills through strategies that reduce classroom jitters, as well as ways to design a streamlined process for lesson planning and grading.

Part I

BREAKING THE
INSTITUTIONAL CODE

CHAPTER 2

Unspoken Structures in the Academic Code

To crack the code of success in an academic workplace, faculty must explicitly understand the culture of the academic community. Faculty development can and should include processes for providing transparency in the academic culture of an institution. If universities are truly committed to improving equity and retaining faculty, they should embrace transparency processes that can reduce implicit bias.

Faculty also must commit to interrogating university structures to clarify and question expectations. Knowledge about university contexts and experiences can lead to a more productive and positive path of faculty development (Lerner, Bowers, Geldhof, Gestsdóttir, & DeSouza et al., 2012; Oppedal & Toppelberg, 2016; Osher, Cantor, Berg, Steyer, & Rose, 2018). Gathering information on an institution's academic code can enable faculty to assess when an institution is not a fit with personal values and purpose (discussed in Chapter 4, "Agency"). Such information can be used to strategically choose when to fit into institutional norms and when to challenge them. Thus, the information in this chapter can be used during the job search process, during the first years on a job to learn the rules of success, and also as a process of discernment of when it is time to move on to another institution.

Research indicates that removing the barriers of transition and socialization to academic jobs must focus on role clarity (Griffin, 2020). This concept captures the actions needed to find success in academia. Agency (see Chapter 4) is related to the mastery of role clarity. Social acceptance and belonging (see Chapter 6) are connected to feeling welcome to a position (Bauer, Bodner, Erdogan, Truxillo, & Tucker, et 2007). Early-career scholars are less confident in the skills needed to find success (Austin, Sorcinelli, & McDaniels, 2007; Rice, Sorcinelli, & Austin, 2000; Sorcinelli & Austin, 2006).

For academics, step one of breaking the academic code is becoming a detective of one's own institutions. Some academics want to thrive in their current environment; others want to move to another university and therefore must learn the rules of other institutions as well. For example, a postdoctoral student accepts a position at an institution with a heavy teaching load but hopes to find a position at a research-focused institution instead. This faculty member is following two academic codes at once—spending days teaching heavy loads and evenings submitting articles for publication while continuing the job search.

IDENTIFYING CODIFIED STRUCTURES

This chapter discusses components of the academic code—including the rules, the norms, and the unspoken biases of institutions (Scott, 2013). Step one begins with understanding the codified rules and regulations. Read those boring documents, often written in hard-to-follow language. They contain important information related to classroom teaching, sabbatical leave, promotion and tenure processes, and more. Attend orientation programs and faculty-development seminars to learn about policies. Ask a lot of questions. Partner with colleagues to share information. And seek out a range of sources to confirm data.

These written documents and formal seminars will not be enough. It will also be important to explicitly interview and ask others to share what they know about how the institution works. Through an iterative process of such conversations, it is possible to piece together a more complete understanding of both written and unwritten expectations.

Key informants can help with this process. These individuals within an institution possess deep knowledge of rules and regulations. Key informants can share what is valued, how conflict is handled, the meetings one must attend, and what responsibilities can be redirected. They also can explain the history behind how universities interpret regulations, such explaining why policies are enforced harshly. These shifts could be due to financial audits, lawsuits, and accreditation processes. I define two types of institutional experts: rule-followers and confidants.

Rule-followers. The first kind of informant is the rule-following expert who knows exactly what the rules are and expects everyone to follow them. These individuals are often found in budget and finance offices as well as human resources offices. They provide detailed, technical answers. For example, they can explain what reimbursements are permitted for travel. They can describe what is contained in permanent records, including formal complaints or grievances.

Confidants. The second type of institutional expert is a person with deep institutional knowledge who can help with ethical dilemmas and complicated problems—the kind that the straight code of the rules does not fully resolve. These experts are skilled at understanding the difference between the hard lines of rules in a culture and the gray spaces. They possess a creativity for crafting solutions for the greater good by piecing together resources and less known aspects of the culture.

An administrator at my university, whose formal title is focused on multicultural affairs, could instead have the informal title of "miracle worker." I have turned to her when I found a student suffering with mental health issues but couldn't arrange an appointment at the psychological services; . . . when a student had a fire at their apartment and was living on a friend's couch; when a student was struggling with such great conflicts at home that they couldn't focus on their schoolwork; . . . when a student couldn't pay their tuition because their father had lost his job.

NORMATIVE PROCESSES—THE CULTURE

"Normative processes" are the unwritten aspects of the institutional culture that are easily identified and discussed (Scott, 2013). Day-to-day activities of universities may not look like what the rule books say. These informal processes may have little logical relationship to the cultural rules (Meyer & Rowan, 1997). Some norms are easily discussed, and others are present but hard to articulate, including the rituals that connect the days and weeks, such as monthly department meetings, the annual holiday potluck, and the extent to which people work in their offices or elsewhere. These unwritten, but known, rules also include who holds longstanding grudges against one another and therefore should not serve on the same committees.

Normative processes also include ways in which conflict is tolerated. Some cultures avoid conflict, whereas others embrace and engage in discussion across difference regularly in meetings (Rockquemore & Laszloffy, 2008). Some cultures openly embrace diversity, and others say they do, though norms say otherwise. Normative processes can privilege dominant culture over other cultures. They include expectations of asserting authority, such as tone, language, eye contact, and comfort with controversy. Normative processes are what one learns first on a job interview when speaking to people and walking the halls of an academic department.

Institutions send lots of signs during an interview process to prospective candidates. These signs can discourage women and underrepresented minority faculty from choosing to work at these universities. Signals, big and little, of a safe and respectful environment are noticed and valued.

When Nina was on the market for her first academic position, she was granted interviews at two universities. Nina had a two-month-old baby. Both universities offered to fly her baby and a caregiver with her to the interviews.

Nina explained that she still would need 20-minute breaks every 3 hours to express her milk. She also needed a private room to do so and a refrigerator to store the milk.

At the first university, Nina arrived to find that her schedule had no breaks at all—other than a short break at 3:00—"when you could go and see your baby." She responded firmly, while remaining as friendly as possible, that her request was a medical issue and not a need to "see" her child.

With great sighing and conveying a sense that she was creating a huge inconvenience, the university agreed to rearrange her schedule. The older White man on the search committee who escorted her through the trip would step out of his own office every 3 hours and let her use his space to express the milk while he waited outside the door. He was trying to be helpful, but she found the situation very unnerving.

Later that evening at dinner with the dean (a White male) and the associate dean (a White female), the dean said to her, "Young moms don't tend to do so well in academia." The associate dean at that point began choking on her steak and spent the rest of the meal trying to make up for the illegal comment of her colleague.

Nina got a clear picture of that culture during the visit—nothing on the website would have clarified the implicit biases within the culture of that university. It was not a family-friendly department, nor was it a woman-friendly department. She thankfully had learned those constraints before accepting a position.

At the second university interview, the staff assistant called Nina ahead of time to confirm that the breaks in her schedule would be sufficient. On the day of the interview, she was shown a private room to pump and a kitchen to refrigerate the milk. She was even granted enough time between meetings that she could walk back across the street to either pump or nurse in her hotel room. The White female department head at the time joked, "Just label that milk well—the older male professors in this department might think it's coffee creamer!" The joke put her at ease and signaled an awareness of the work left to do in the department regarding bias, but it was also a signal of support from her future supervisor, who made her feel that she would be fully supported. The department head's warmth and support helped Nina to feel that this university could be a welcoming space. She also perceived her future department head to be a potential mentor.

Nina received offers from both universities and felt the choice to select the second university was easy.

A note about this vignette: When I had a colleague read it, she said, "You need to change that vignette. It is too similar to Jada's experience. It will be clear it was her"—except it wasn't Jada's story at all. The story may sound extreme, but it was actually so common that multiple women thought that it was their story being told.

COGNITIVE PROCESSES: HIDDEN BELIEFS AND STRUCTURES

Cognitive processes exist *sub rosa*—they are not spoken, yet they are very much expected (Scott, 2013). Uncovering cognitive processes is truly about "getting into people's heads"—figuring out the criteria being used that are hard to articulate.

Each year when my new graduate students begin their first semester, I encouraged my new advisees to take my senior graduate students out for coffee to ask what it's like to be a student in the program, and especially what it's like to work with me. Although I can articulate some guidelines and expectations for what I expect of my students, I have my own blind spots about what I really expect. My experienced students could better articulate the unspoken rules working with me than I could directly.

These *sub rosa* cognitive thoughts, habits, and actions are also the reason why therapists, counselors, and coaches are often an important part of the path to self-growth and improvement. Removing the stigma of mental health support is a part of the process of changing the structure of academia. Taking responsibility to seek help from professionals allows work on blind spots that can cause the most damage. Sometimes the issue that is most critical is the very one that the psyche refuses to see without the help of trusted, helpful professionals. Others can identify patterns of action that have been buried inside.

IMPLICIT BIAS AND PRIVILEGE AS COGNITIVE STRUCTURES

At their worst, cognitive structures can be the source of prejudice. Implicit bias results from cognitive processes. Even people who believe in equity and who affirm the value of a diverse faculty unconsciously behave in discriminatory ways. Qualifications, training, and intentions do not eliminate cognitive processes embedded into interactions that cause pain and injury and create disparities. It is the job of every person to acknowledge and humbly work to make these unconscious actions visible—to interrogate oneself and do better.

Bias includes treating the same behaviors differently. Research about individuals in the workplace has demonstrated that identical behaviors are perceived differently based on the person's race and gender. One study simply changed the name in a case study from male to female. By doing so, perceptions of likeability and pushiness dramatically changed (Martin, 2007).

Microaggressions still occur, even by people who are consciously trying to be equitable. Often, people cannot see their own forms of bias even when looking, and it is necessary for others to recognize and voice concern. Bias can be explicit discrimination—and it can also be an unequal treatment of individuals based on their identities and diversity of perspectives, rather than on their capabilities to complete their jobs. The greater the forms of privilege held, the greater the likelihood of engaging in microaggression and implicit bias. Privilege consists of the intersections (Crenshaw, 2017) of one's identity that are in the majority. Privilege is having the ability to choose not to pay attention. It is the choice to avoid discomfort even when others are uncomfortable.

Privileged identities require much less energy because the explicit and implicit norms of cultures embrace them as taken-for-granted. The extra energy needed to not be in the majority is taxing. White people may spend very little time during the day thinking about how they are White and the ways in which that will affect interactions with others and with institutions. Cisgender individuals may not feel the need to clarify pronouns because the assumptions will fit their needs. Able-bodied people do not need to plan ahead to make sure they can access a meeting room. All of these assumptions are forms of privilege.

Faculty who have identities not privileged as dominant in their universities—including faculty of color, women, LGBTQ, disabled, and non-binary individuals—face greater layers of bias and struggle in achieving success in academia. Underrepresented faculty face issues of bias much more regularly in academic institutions. Far too often, underrepresented faculty are questioned as to whether they actually conducted their own research and about their contribution in coauthored materials, and are given no credit for introducing ideas in meetings (Griffin, Bennett, & Harris, 2013; Rockquemore & Laszloffy, 2008; Seltzer, 2015). Underrepresented faculty also face *hypervisibility*—a feeling that they are being watched for appropriateness and a need to exceed the successes of other faculty in order to be accepted (Griffin et al., 2013). Underrepresented faculty experience threats to research credibility and classroom authority (Bavishi, Madera, & Hebl, 2010; Ford, 2011; Moore, Acosta, Perry, & Edwards, 2010; Perry, Moore, Edwards, Acosta, & Frey, 2009; Pittman, 2010a) and the devaluing of teaching and scholarship due to the frequent focus on equity-related topics (Garrison-Wade, Diggs, Estrada, & Galindo, 2012; Jayakumar, Howard, Allen, & Han, 2009).

Research documents ways in which faculty of color face greater basic concerns of threats (Kelly & McCann, 2014) and unfair treatment during promotion and tenure processes (Collaborative on Academic Careers in Higher Education, 2007). Faculty of color also face lower teaching evaluations relative to White counterparts (Garrison-Wade et al., 2012; McGowan, 2000; Smith & Anderson, 2005; Vargas, 2002). Faculty of color also face microaggressions—acts of disregard from a lack of consciousness of White superiority that can lead to slights, inappropriate questions and jokes, and negative stereotypes—and they must assert the validity and strength of their research and prove that they earned their appointments (Griffin, Pifer,

Humphrey, & Hazelwood, 2011; Johnsrud & Sadao, 1998; McKay, 1997; Solórzano, Allen, & Carroll, 2002; Stanley, 2006). Research also documents double standards in perception of issues such as collaboration and coauthoring, with White scholars being described as team players and faculty of color being described as needy and dependent on others and even questioned as to whether their work is truly their own.

Women also experience a biased climate (Greene, Stockard, Lewis, & Richmond, 2010; Kelly & McCann, 2014; Marschke, Laursen, Nielsen, & Dunn-Rankin, 2007) and gender inequity (Amey, 1996; Gardner, 2013; Rosser, 2004). The COVID-19 pandemic exacerbated these barriers as faculty lost child care at the same time that research was difficult to conduct. The widening gender gap caused by the lack of child care during the pandemic will be felt for years following the end of the pandemic.

Underrepresented faculty are also assigned heavy teaching and service responsibilities due to an "identity tax" (Griffin, 2020; Griffin, Bennett, & Harris, 2013, Garrison-Wade et al., 2012; Gardner, 2013; Kelly & Fetridge, 2012; Kulis, Sicotte, & Colins, 2002; Misra, Lundquist, Holmes, & Agiomavritis, 2011; Museus, Maramba, & Teranishi, 2013). That is, these individuals are often asked to serve on diversity committees and to *be* the diversity within committees. Underrepresented students seek mentoring from faculty who identify similar to themselves because they do not feel they are getting sufficient guidance elsewhere. Research on these issues has largely focused on faculty of color and women in academia; greater research is needed to document and advocate for the broader range of ways in which diverse faculty with a range of intersectional identities leads to disparity.

CREATING AN INCLUSIVE AND WELCOMING CLIMATE

As one strategy to improve climate issues and address implicit bias, universities may form bias response teams that monitor climate issues and also receive reports of prejudice from faculty, students, and staff and have educational conversations with the subjects of the reports. These teams rarely have the power to discipline potential violations and cannot stop free speech of faculty or students. However, such committees can refer deeper issues to law enforcement and university disciplinary panels (Miller, Guida, Smith, Ferguson, & Medina, 2018).

Such approaches have been critiqued for not having enough scale or resources to address concerns and improve climate. Leadership on such teams also falls on a spectrum of opposing demands of investigating reported violations and managing negative press from potential cases. Researchers also caution that this one strategy cannot replace a broader goal of creating a welcoming climate for all faculty and students (Miller, Guida, Smith, & Ferguson, 2018).

With most research-focused universities being predominantly White, research shows a consistent experience of underrepresented faculty facing isolation, racism, discrimination, and bias due to race, ethnicity, gender, and sexual orientation (Garrison-Wade et al., 2012; Gutiérrez y Mus, Niemann, Kelly & McCann, 2014; Museus et al., 2013; Zambrana, Ray, Espino, Castro, Douthirt Cohen, & Eliason, 2015). Underrepresented faculty also receive less overt support and experience a lack of mentoring and academic socialization (Diggs, Garison-Wade, Estrada, & Galindo, 2009; Kelly & McMann, 2014; Stanley, 2006; Stanley & Lincoln, 2005; Tierney & Bensimon, 1996).

Anisa, a pre-tenured professor at a Research I institution, came to me after receiving a negative third-year review (a mid-course review that happens before tenure at her institution). Although the committee expressed concerns about her publishing capabilities, they were equally concerned about what they described as her lack of collegiality. They cited her failure to attend the program's weekly symposia and seminars. They pointed to her not having any current doctoral students. They also commented that she was rarely sitting in her office.

Anisa had received a fellowship that gave her a leave from university responsibilities that previous year, including from service and teaching responsibilities. Although such honors are usually praised, her nonattendance at faculty meetings during her fellowship was viewed as a lack of commitment to the program. The reduced teaching load also meant that doctoral students did not know much about her and therefore did not ask her to join their committees.

Furthermore, Anisa was cross-appointed to two different programs. Each of these programs had its own set of meetings and symposia. She struggled politically to discern which program's expectations mattered the most for her future. It was not until she received her negative review that she understood which of the subcultures of the university was truly in charge of her fate. That was the culture that she needed to master.

I coached Anisa on identifying her allies within the university. She had to seek out formal channels for redress but also learn about supportive and sympathetic leaders. She sought colleagues who were having similar struggles to identify possible patterns of behavior. She looked within to reaffirm her own sense of worth and purpose related to her work. She reaffirmed her ethics and what she considered to be quality work. Collaborations within the university and beyond helped to affirm the shared value of her work and to keep her focused on producing that work, regardless of whether she would remain at that university or move on to another.

Anisa's case raises the decision points at which one might need to decide when to question the policies that are harming success for underrepresented

> ### DISCERNING WHEN TO CHALLENGE A DISCRIMINATORY SITUATION
>
> - What lines of integrity and voices in your scholarship are non-negotiable?
> - What audiences would be more receptive to your work in the short term?
> - What stances/actions/content are you willing to delay until after promotion/tenure?
> - What allies could help you navigate between the non-negotiable and the contention caused by your work?

faculty. The text box offers some queries to help faculty discern when it is time to challenge and question and when it is time to wait.

ADDRESSING GRIEVANCES

It is critical to understand the courses of action available when grievances occur. When raising grievances, faculty must clarify their intentions. Consider what could be requested from a formal process. Options tend to be redress, a space to be heard, or a change in policy for the future. Understand that the official roles within a university vary in terms of who and how they can provide support.

Create a plan of action. Develop an explicit plan of learning as much as possible about the actual expectations of the university. Gather information through documents and interviews with others. Set up meetings with the senior faculty, ask for feedback, and inquire as to which sets of meetings are critical for success.

Find the ombudsperson. Ombudspeople are trained as mediators. They offer a space of strict confidentiality. It is the job of the ombudsperson to help an individual understand the pathways for recourse and, when appropriate, to bring together two sides of a conflict for mediation. Talking with the ombudsperson is a good way to share concerns when emotions are running high. Ombudspeople can help clarify emotions and to define the intention of the involved parties.

Know the formal channels for redress. Understand the regulative processes for receiving support. Know who is in charge of support of receiving and acting on faculty concerns. Larger universities may have iterative processes of support, so finding the many pockets of potential allies or information is important.

Work collectively when possible. It may be more effective for faculty to approach authority collectively. For example, if a male professor is consistently speaking derogatively and decisively toward women, a group of senior and junior female faculty might request a meeting to speak to the dean collectively. By providing multiple sources of evidence, multiple types of experience, and iterative documentation of concern, faculty can attract greater attention to their concerns.

Document and save evidence. When faculty engages in a grievance process, it is critical to document in writing as possible. Ask for information. Learn what one's rights are. Document any evidence that could be provided to the bias—even if this information is saved for later. Save emails, voicemails, text messages, and written communication. Request communication in ways that it can be documented as well during difficult situations.

THE INSTITUTION OF TENURE

Tenure is a rite of passage designed to socialize faculty to institutional legitimacy by mastering the spoken and unspoken rules (Lawrence, Celis, & Ott, 2014; Suchman, 1995). Tenure serves as a gatekeeping practice that acculturates faculty through a stepwise evaluation process. Barriers to gaining tenure include collegial relations, overall organizational climate, the quality of feedback, and access to resources (Ambrose, Huston, & Norman, 2005; August & Waltman, 2004; Tierney & Bensimon, 1996). Experiences of the tenure and promotion process vary according to gender (O'Meara, 2002; Rosser, 2004), race (Jayakumar et al., 2009; Ponjuan, Conley, & Trower, 2011), disciplinary affiliation (Rice & Sorcinelli, 2002), and years on the tenure track (Barnes & Mertz, 2010; Ponjuan et al., 2011).

When preparing materials for promotion, faculty should aim to complete the process early enough that those materials can be shared with people who have previously served on promotion and tenure committees. These experienced people have an eye for what a committee looks for as compared to the written rules. They can identify potential problems or insufficient information. Any awkward feelings of asking for feedback at this level are far less painful than being denied promotion for lack of preparation or savvy in how to communicate work experiences in the dossier. Get opinions from different kinds of people, with varying social statuses, with varying demographics, social statuses, and experiences with the university. If information conflicts, get more information and be aware of the range of expectations as much as a single standard. That too is information.

As an assistant professor, I identified three female full professors in my department to mentor me through the tenure process. All of them had either served on the collegewide promotion and tenure committee or had worked in the university's administration. Every couple of years, I shared my progress on my work with them. With a year to go before making the case for my promotion, I had each give a close read of my CV to identify potential holes in my case. One colleague noted that I was not showing how I was a national figure. She urged me to document any press call, newspaper mention, and accolade. "You are not bragging," she said. "You are showing you are an expert. Men would not have trouble sharing their accolades."

Research indicates that faculty retention policies for underrepresented faculty should focus on providing effective feedback, quality mentoring, instructional support, and equitable treatment—and especially during tenure and promotion processes (American Council on Education, 2001; Lawrence et al., 2014). In contrast, negative experiences with the tenure process can lead to low job satisfaction and less engagement in the university, including citizenship behavior (Cameron & Hyer, 2010; Dooris & Guidos, 2006; Huston, Norman, & Ambrose, 2007; O'Meara, 2002).

The culture of universities in some nations constructs faculty evaluation as a quantified process, with faculty expected to use workload calculators to demonstrate contribution. Faculty at these universities are given points for activities performed, from publishing to serving on committees. These points affect ongoing job performance reviews and the future allocation of teaching and service responsibilities. These calculators can be ineffective rubrics for measuring a broad range of impact. They have been criticized by faculty worldwide for placing limits on credit for activities, such as a maximum limit on grading hours.

On the other side of the spectrum, dissatisfaction with the process in the United States focuses on role ambiguity about what is considered "quality work" in a dossier for promotion and tenure. The definition of quality is rarely written down in university policy. Although the handbook may offer general guidelines, faculty will often answer "It depends," since quality scholarship can embody a range of styles. Related ambiguous words in the academy include *rigorous, innovative,* and *excellence*—all of these words are social constructs (Matthew, 2016).

Tenure and promotion dossiers have a deeper set of expectations than what is written in the guidelines. Tenure processes must accommodate a range of hiring expectations, including specific departmental needs, teaching loads, and research genres. These expectations vary in how work is presented in the materials, what supplemental work should be included, and how to present data. For tenure dossiers, most universities hesitate to give a magic number of publications necessary for success in the promotion process. Although two to three peer-reviewed publications might be the average, scholars might write only a few publications, but they are considered critical to their field. Another scholar might publish 20 articles, but the quality

of work is viewed as thin and insufficient. The best way to understand the
tenure rules is to interview as many people as possible who have served on
the tenure committees. Ask as many people as possible. The text box offers
some suggested questions to ask colleagues.

Try to find dossiers of similar quality and scope of work. Request dossiers
from people with similar types of research and teaching loads, and within
the same program or college. Looking at several examples can help to distill
the unspoken rules as much as the written and to gain a sense of quality. This
strategy does not work if the faculty member is the first person to go up for
tenure in a department in a decade, or the department head is brand-new.
In such cases, ask if someone in power could share examples of what they
consider to be quality work.

Building relationships with senior faculty. Research indicates that junior
faculty without senior faculty mentors believe they are disadvantaged in
tenure processes and more generally (Cawyer & Friedrich, 1998; Lawrence
et al., 2014; Philip & Hendry, 2000). Lack of collaboration on research
with senior colleagues is also viewed as hampering potential research productivity (Sorcinelli, 1992).

Junior faculty lacking such relationships describe senior faculty as preoc-
cupied or disinterested (Ambrose, Norman, & Huston, 2007). Relationships
with department chairs are particularly important hierarchical relationships that are correlated with promotion and tenure decisions (Ambrose
et al., 2005; Gmelch & Schuh, 2004), and chair turnover is particularly

QUESTIONS TO CLARIFY THE ACADEMIC CODE AT A UNIVERSITY

- What is the number of peer-reviewed articles and books needed for promotion?
- Does the number of publications expected vary based on the quality of the journals?
- What "counts" as published research and what does not?
- What expectations exist for the percentage of single-authored publications?
- Do publications count from before my arrival at this institution?
- What is expected in terms of impact/reputation nationally? Internationally?
- How much service is expected at the department, university, and national levels?
- Should I elaborate on issues that are anomalies?
- What level of funding and grant success is expected for promotion?

detrimental to junior faculty (Ambrose et al., 2005; August & Waltman, 2004). Chairs can mediate workload, resource allocation, inclusion in decision-making, and distribution of teaching and service load (Ambrose et al., 2005; Gmelch & Schuh, 2004; Misra et al., 2011).

RECOMMENDATIONS FOR UNIVERSITIES

- Design cohorts of assistant professors who can work together to build their dossiers. Have senior faculty with a range of backgrounds meet with the cohorts to describe their career processes and to provide insights on the promotion and tenure process at that institution.
- Hire coaches to support faculty who struggle with their tenure and promotion. Invest in targeted, intensive support while there is still time to improve writing productivity and explain the unspoken rules more clearly.
- Improve support during the second year of the tenure process. Any setbacks from the beginning of a tenure-track process tend to be visible the second year, when publications are (or are not) accepted. Universities focusing on the second year offer a series of activities such as determining what progress should look like at year 2, writing for publication workshops, reviewing and learning from teaching evaluations, and learning how to choose service wisely (Tulley, 2018).
- Conduct a needs assessment of mentoring and review practices experienced by faculty. Use research-based practice to improve mentoring and review policies. Provide ongoing professional development to department heads on how to provide effective mentoring and feedback.
- Clarify the intention of promotional policies—which are in service of supporting faculty? Which are really about protecting the university rather than supporting faculty? Where can a balance be struck, and how can these decisions be more transparent?
- Assess mechanisms that faculty can use to raise concerns about support and feedback. Consult with best practices on bias and supporting faculty of color, and make these conversations transparent and collaborative across departments.

CHAPTER 3

The Inner Critic

Many people struggle with having an inner critic that says the mean and awful retorts. The inner critic can lead to imposter syndrome. It can lead to a loss of hope and create feelings of doom. It is a voice that is so terrible that it speaks words to oneself that would never be said to a loved one (or even an unliked colleague).

Tasha struggled with finishing her dissertation proposal. Every time she sat down to write, an imaginary old, White, male professor would sit on her shoulder with her and tell her she would never amount to anything. This awful specter was an actual teacher that she had had in her younger years—a reflection of the smallest version of herself that returned when she doubted herself.

It helps to know that inner critics live in everyone—a few, in fact: one for relationships, one for career, one for social situations. Notice them. Identify them. Be curious about them. Do not be angry or fuel the fear. Laugh. Rise above.

Social science explains where this awful voice comes from. Applying the research on institutional theory to concepts in coaching frameworks, we can understand that taken-for-granted institutional messaging resides in minds as inner critics. The inner critic takes in the biases from the world and places them inside.

The warnings of inner critics may have been important in previous times but are no longer valid. Perhaps they come from times of physical or emotional danger. They set off unresolved alarm bells in newer, safer situations. Thank these alarm bells when they ring. Acknowledge the purpose they may have served previously. Then intentionally notice the skills and the supports available that make them no longer necessary.

Despite receiving a prestigious fellowship to attend graduate school and obtaining a 4.0 in her coursework, Eileen felt that her dissertation defense was a rough ride. Her committee members were more critical than she expected. They raised doubts about the rigor of her findings, claiming that she was speaking more from advocacy than from the data itself. She managed to pass her dissertation after multiple revisions.

Eileen found a plum tenure-track position at a university with supportive colleagues. She successfully published on new research that she was conducting with great collaborators, but she struggled to publish out of her dissertation. She felt blocked and paralyzed. Every time she tried, she would hear the voices of her committee in her head, telling her that her work did not match up to the standard that they had expected.

I worked with Eileen to make a list of the positive feedback she had received about this same work—feedback from conference presentations, job interviews, and collaborators. She displayed these affirmations of her work so that she could remember that many appreciated her work. Collecting enough positive messages helped drown out the messages of the committee members who instilled doubt in her abilities.

SHAME TRIGGERS WITH THE INNER CRITIC

Shame increases the possibility of getting stuck in setbacks. Instead of focusing on cleaning up the problems, we allow shame to cause a focus on self-judgment and despair. Brown (2018, p. 126) defines shame as "the intensely painful feeling or experience of believing that we are flawed and unworthy of love, belonging, and connection." Shame amplifies the inner critic voice of "I will never be a good enough scholar."

Brown explains that shame can build armor as an effort to protect oneself from potential harm. These supposed forms of protection can also lead to physical issues because it absorbs the negativity inside the body rather than setting it free. Singer (2007) explains this armoring process with the metaphor of getting punctured by a thorn. One can pull the thorn out or hold onto the thorn and expend enormous energy protecting the thorn. One can avoid letting anything touch the thorn to avoid the pain of the initially small wound. One can create great protective mechanisms to preserve and avoid the thorn. One can be brave enough to face the thorn head-on— consider the feedback, and then set it free.

By creating awareness of thorns, we can hope to strengthen the positive sources of inspiration, energy, and support. The next section illustrates how to identify values and to build confidence and purpose.

Maxie wanted to be a writer and a life coach. In the past, she had blogged for herself. Those blogs poured out of her. Now that she had set a goal of having a career of being a writer, the joy of writing had evaporated. She found herself spending 18 to 20 hours per blog. In her mind, her writing had to be perfect.

When I asked her why she was spending so much time on each blog, she told me, "Writers work hard. They don't do half-ass. Eighty percent of people fail. I have to be the twenty percent."

I asked, "Where is that message coming from?"

She replied, "The writers I love the most—Anne Lamott, I think!"

"Anne Lamott writes just the opposite," I countered. "She talks about writing 'shitty first drafts' to get the words out onto the page. Who really is the voice in your head?"

She paused a moment and laughed, "An infomercial for weight loss, saying I can't skip one day of exercise. That's what's in my head, making me feel guilty about my writing. A commercial shaming me into buying their products."

By finding the source of inner critics, we can get to the root of the negative message—much like pulling a dandelion out by the root instead of just pulling the flower, which will quickly grow back again. Maxie's inner critic was not even drawn from writing experiences. She was transferring a shaming experience she had from another part of her life to her writing. By noting the source of her critic, she was able to distance herself from it. She pulled the thorn out instead of protecting it, as Singer would say. Her writing flowed again, and she learned to remove even greater thorns. Within 6 months, she also stopped drinking and started a new job that aligned more closely to her values.

FINDING THE INNER CRITIC IN THE BODY

Clients often ask me how to know when the inner critic is posing as inner truth. This struggle can be especially problematic with academics, who are trained to overuse their brains. My answer: "Is the voice lifting you up or tearing you down?" An inner critic voice tends to feel harsh, mean, negative, and binary, and focuses on "not enough" (Mohr, 2015). Inner wisdom does not seek to destroy (Tolle, 2006).

Another tactic for discerning authentic inner wisdom is to tap into the body, which possesses innate ways of knowing. An inner critic voice often has some of these properties: mean, harsh, stuck in binaries, judging and demeaning, repetitive, persistent, draws on previous failures, sounds like critical people from the past, creates feelings of anxiety and worry, and/or sounds like perfectionism (adapted from Mohr, 2015).

Tapping into knowledge below the chins—in hearts and guts—can be a great way of discerning what is deeper truth. The truth from the inside is much bigger than cognitive processes. In fact, the body gives great insights that tend to be taken for granted.

Consider how different parts of the bodies help to know truth. Hands may shake during an important conversation. A stomach may twinge when in love. Truth comes from a "gut feeling." The throat constricts when silenced.

These sensations are driven by the stimulation of the *vagus nerve*, the largest component of the autonomic nervous system, which communicates with the lungs, heart, stomach, liver, pancreas, and gut. Called the "soul nerve" (Menakem, 2017), the vagus nerve informs consciousness in ways just beginning to be understood. It is also part of the process that tells the body when to fight, flight, or freeze.

Any of these signals are out of conscious awareness. With practice, attending to gut feelings can help discern the messages the body is sending, as well as intentionally calm messages to reduce stress response.

While teaching a room of entrepreneurial leaders to tap into their inner wisdom, I asked the large conference room:

"Close your eyes. Find your feet. Feel grounded in the earth. Ask your feet what information they have to share."

One person shared that her foot shot straight up in the air—almost out of her control. She shared that she had been considering relocating for a long time from her hometown. She felt sure that her foot was telling her that she no longer wanted to be grounded in this current place. She had been trying to get the courage to relocate for years. The trouble, she said, was her "mind" kept telling her all of the reasons that leaving would be irresponsible. The inner critic had taken over her head space. But her feet still had the wisdom to tell her what she needed to know.

STEPPING AWAY FROM THE INNER CRITIC

One way to reduce the harm of the inner critic is to create a distance between one's sense of self and the voice of the inner critic within. It helps to speak to it and recognize that it is a voice separate from one's own self. The skill of removing negative thinking is also called "disputing" (Seligman, 1991). It is possible to disagree with negative thoughts and focus on optimistic ways of thinking. The impact is felt within the body instantly. Responding with anger will just fuel the negativity. Challenging it will make it strong. Anger feeds it and breeds fear rather than compassion.

When I coached Claire, a mom with a full-time job, to create a persona for her inner critic, she chose the name "Shoulda Woulda Coulda," because she always felt she could be doing more in some role in her life, and she especially felt like she was not doing enough as a mom.

I also had her draw her inner critic. She scribbled a woman with long curly hair like herself, but the hair was sticking out like the Bride of Frankenstein filled with electricity. Her inner critic was filled with frenzy . . . telling her she should always be doing more . . . telling her that she was not worthy to be cared for or to take care of herself.

She had embodied the effects of perfectionism over time. The external voices of what "mom" and a "professor" looked like were haunting her. By externalizing and personifying these demons in her head—playfully—she could help separate her own passions and purpose from stereotypes and false expectations.

By personifying the inner critic, we can much more easily send it off with love. It is easier to talk to the inner critic playfully when it shows up. This process helps to distance the critic. It is a foreign thing stuck in our head, and we can politely ask it to leave when it shows up. Don't get caught up in emotion or get mad at it or being there.

One of my clients put a garden gnome on her desk. She calls him Gnome Chomsky. When the demons are getting the best of her, she talks to the garden gnome. She thanks him for his concern but tells him that his harsh comments are no longer helpful.

Rather than focusing on anger and fear, meet the inner critic with gratitude. Acknowledge that it is trying to protect. Perhaps this behavior even created conditions that led to transformation. But the protection no longer serves. Be grateful for its intentions. Switch from focusing on a manic tone to a calm tone . . . from running the same "tapes" of criticisms to taking a baby step forward . . . from edicts and judgment to curiosity . . . from blame and shame to comfort and learning (Mohr, 2015).

The text box provides a process for meeting the inner critic. The way to defeat the inner critic is to separate it from the true self. Give that critic personality. Draw the inner critic. Make a collage of images of it. Find a funny representation of it to remember that it is separate from the true self.

RUMINATION: THE INNER CRITIC ON REPEAT

One version of the inner critic struggle is the replay of "tapes in our heads"—to review difficult moments over and over, as if doing so will change the outcome or allow us to say the "right" thing this time.

John tended to ruminate while walking his dog. He found himself in the gorgeous Pennsylvania woods near his house, and instead of noticing this moment, often the most beautiful of his day, he found his mind wanting to drift back to the moments of his life that have been unsettling.

Rumination causes obsession over these struggles and keeps minds stuck in the past. Replaying difficult times never changes them. Rumination just keeps us feeling miserable. Ongoing rumination raises anxiety, which interferes with problem solution.

Stepping away from rumination can begin by noticing the behavior and detaching from the emotions that it sparks. Brach (2019) refers to the process as RAIN—Recognizing the emotion, Allow its presence. Investigate with

---

INNER CRITIC EXERCISES

- Choose a name for your inner critic.
- Describe your inner critic with rich detail.
- Sketch your inner critic (without judging your sketch!).
- When does this inner critic show up the most?
- What actions/strategies will you use to lovingly send it away?

---

curiosity, Nurture with compassion. The process acknowledges the feeling but meets it with compassion rather than rejection. Catching the repetition of the thought process is the first step.

The next step is to meet that recognition with kindness, not shame. Just note that "There it is again." With conscious awareness, exit the "negative memory network" (Wehrenberg, 2016) in which negativity feeds upon itself and grows. Rumination tends to be triggered by mood. Pulling away from the repetitive tapes helps us take in the present moment.

Michelle requested coaching because she felt like she could not step away from negative thoughts. She thought she was practicing self-care by taking a walk in the woods with her dog every day. But once she brought herself into this quiet, beautiful space, her mind started replaying tapes of mistakes she had made and unresolved conflicts. She would rehash arguments, and people who had mistreated her would loom in her mind. Then she would get angry with herself for thinking these feelings.

I worked with Michelle to gently notice these feelings and to focus on positive emotions as she consciously brought herself back to the present moment. Michelle chose to do so by focusing on her senses. She would say out loud, "I am walking my dog. I hear the crunch of the leaves beneath my feet. I smell the turn of the weather to autumn. I can see the sun filtering through the trees. I can feel the cool weather on my face."

She also focused on gratitude for what was working in her life, and especially small moments. Often just a few minutes of being present allowed her to turn away from the past and to enjoy her time in the woods.

Many strategies can help to stop the repeating tapes. Robbins (2017) suggests a similar pattern of disruption by counting backward from 5. Counting backward causes the brain to work a bit harder and shakes off the rumination. Before arriving at 1, we typically find that the repeating tape is cut off.

Another set of research suggests that playing music or singing out loud can also rewire the brain to stop the repeating tapes (Wehrenberg, 2016). In all of these strategies, the goal is to find a grounding in the present moment, to notice the body instead of getting trapped in the mind.

Research also indicates that a regular gratitude practice leads to joy (Brown, 2010). Rather than joyful people feeling grateful, the data indicate the opposite—but a regular process of noticing moments of gratitude from the day builds joy within people. A gratitude practice is most common at the end of the day, listing at least five appreciative moments in the day. The finer-grained and more specific the moments, the better the outcomes.

Listing reasons and causes also deepens the outcomes. Therefore, instead of saying, "I am grateful for my daughter," instead say, "I am grateful that my teenage daughter texted me her excitement about passing her exam *because* it reassures me of the connection between us and that she wanted to share that special moment with me." This fine-grained gratitude practice builds resonance with those special moments.

Through a gratitude practice we have the opportunity to repeat those feelings and moments. This repetition deepens positive neural networks within our brains, thus building the habits of joy, gratitude, peace, and happiness. Reinforcing pathways of joy is time spent when we are not wallowing in our lizard brain, where fear, resentment, and trauma reside.

INNER CRITICS AND STRESS RESPONSE

Neuroscience research using methods such as brain scans have increasingly demonstrated that emotions are chemical reactions that affect every organ of the body. Although academics tend to think of themselves as highly rational, these brain scans show us all to be highly emotional, with the cognitive context lacking great consistency in "controlling" these emotions.

In brains, the actual stressor is separate from the stress. The cognitive brain thinks that if a stressful situation is complete, the moment is over. However, Nagoski and Nagoski (2020) demonstrate that the stress response does not know to stop the emotions of fear, grief, and shame. It is necessary, therefore, to attend to the stress response itself so that it does not become embedded in the body as illness, anxiety, and depression. Nagoski and Nagoski (2020) offer intentional ways of completing a stress response, including breathing work, exercise, laughter, crying, and hugging a loved one.

Trauma is the deepest version of bodies embedding stress responses. When it feels like the inner critic cannot let go and the emotions feel much bigger than an immediate situation at hand, it might signal an underlying trauma. If paralysis, fear, or sadness feels bigger than one can handle, it is an opportunity to work with a helping professional to move through these experiences toward a path of healing.

View these triggers as a gift or recognition of the work that needs to be done. It is only by moving through the dark parts of the soul that it is possible to feel free enough to be the fullest version of oneself. The memories of the trauma will never disappear, but they can become a part of one's history rather than taking hostage of the present. Trauma can stem from many sources. One useful resource for trauma related to racism is the groundbreaking book *My Grandmother's Hands: Racialized Trauma and the Pathway to Mending Our Hearts and Bodies*. The book combines empirical research with practical application to how racism becomes embodied in everyone. Drawing on somatic therapy, author Resmaa Menakem (2017) focuses on the ways in which trauma becomes stuck within bodies. Using mindfulness strategies, the book examines unhealthy reflexive responses to traumatic emotion for Black and White people.

GETTING UNSTUCK FROM WRITER'S BLOCK

The inner critic will draw on perfectionism to freeze the writing process. With publishing so important in academic careers, pushing through writer's block is an essential skill. To step away from perfectionism:

- pause and apply a wider-angle lens to consider the big picture of your work and how this piece of writing fits within your purpose and values,
- identify how this particular piece of writing inspires and excites, and
- assume a stance of play, creativity, and exploration.

Sometimes the block happens after we are fearful of what the reaction of others will be. Acknowledge habits of overpreparation. Talk to the inner critic and plan to submit writing before you feel it is fully ready. Have a colleague read the piece to help to decide if it's ready to submit. Err on submitting when not fully ready rather than holding onto work for too long. Send papers out when they are 80%–90% ready, knowing that they will be coming back for review.

Beyond these bigger pieces, writing can be improved through discipline—creating structures and habits that allow us to push through the doubt.

Break bigger writing projects into chunks. Create 30- to 45-minute writing tasks to make a bigger project feasible. Lamott (2007) describes her stress in writing a book report on birds as a child and her father telling her, "Take it bird by bird." She uses this as a metaphor for all of her writing. Breaking long assigments into smaller tasks makes the work approachable.

Set a timer for 30 minutes. Work without stopping until the timer ends the session. Often this uninterrupted time on the piece is enough to get going again. Otherwise, if nothing else, 30 more minutes have been dedicated to the task than would have been otherwise.

"Draw" to see the connections between ideas. Grab a blank sheet of paper and some colorful markers. Connect all of the ideas together with circles and lines and bubbles. Getting out of a linear structure can help clarify the main ideas. Write using the nondominant hand when feelings of being stuck emerge. Try this task in a new writing space and see what arises.

Incubate fuzzy ideas. If continuing to write is not working, let the idea "incubate." Often this process is needed when ideas feel fuzzy—an idea is there, but it's not well articulated yet. Pose a critical question about the work and then engage in a physical activity. Go on a run. Clean the kitchen. Bake cookies. Even take a nap. While completing the activity of choice, keep the question present in the corner of your mind. See if inspiration sparks. Research shows that incubation can spur creativity and get the writing going again (Medd, 2002). Just be sure to return to writing that day or the day after.

Change space when you are stuck. Physically move to a new location. Work at the office. Work at home. Try out writing in a new cafe with a friend. Or try writing alone in a quiet library. Move the desk near a window—a view of nature can mean greater work satisfaction and well-being (Leather, Pyrgas, Beale, & Lawrence, 1998).

THE CRITIC IN ACADEMIA: PEER REVIEW

The peer review process in academia is also ripe for calling forth the inner critic. A couple of negative reviews can create a never-ending cycle of negative thoughts—a belief that one's work is not valid. Blind feedback from others seems to invite reviewers to speak frankly and not soften concerns. Reviewers can be harsh, rude, and downright nasty.

The transfer to shame in academic writing occurs when shifting from reflecting on the flaws in the piece of writing to flaws within. This shift to owning the setback as a reflection of character is hurtful and even dangerous, and research shows that it is correlated with addiction, violence, and depression (Brown, 2018).

Shame in academic writing turns into perfectionism and ties self-worth to productivity. When "armoring up" occurs in the writing process, it creates a defensiveness that prohibits creativity and innovation (Brown, 2018). It leads to playing it safe and not taking risks in scholarship. It leads to feelings of unworthiness and rejection, and it discourages vulnerability and the risk-taking necessary to advance scholarship. It leads my clients to endlessly wordsmith and edit papers that have been ready for submission months before. It leads to important work never being released for feedback for fear of what the response might be.

All academics receive a scathing review at some point in their careers. They experience a reviewer who misses the point of the piece or who turns from careful analysis of the article to widespread slander of character and ability. The difficulty of the review process requires a set of targeted strategies for overcoming the critics.

Upon receiving any peer review, our first step should be to read it once, and then put it away for a few days; let the positive and negative feedback season. Then return to the feedback later that week with a mind open to suggestions for improvement. The text box provides a short list of questions to consider when receiving feedback.

In her first month on the job as an assistant professor, Janelle sent the best slice of her dissertation off to the top journal in her field. The editors refused to even send her work out for peer review, claiming that no one would be interested in her topic.

Since the rejection was a disagreement of the value of the topic and not a critique of flawed design, I coached Janelle to consider publishing to be a game. The publishing process is a game. Publishing can be like a tennis match in which balls are coming across the net at rapid speed. Lob them back, as quickly as possible. Learn what you can from the feedback. Develop stronger scholarship from it. And then bravely send it back out for others to read. You "win" if you are the last lob. No one knows how long the rally continues after the game is over.

By quickly volleying it back out, we talked about not allowing the feedback to get stuck inside of her—it was a disagreement of genre. She needed to find her audience.

Janelle quickly sent the manuscript to the number-two top journal in her field. They accepted the piece with minor revisions, and it has remained her

---

JOURNALING QUESTIONS ON RECEIVING FEEDBACK

- Think of a time that feedback has been helpful in strengthening your argument and writing. What did the feedback look like? What were the qualities of how it was presented?
- What type of feedback instead stops you in your tracks? What patterns of difficult feedback tend to trigger your inner critic? What alternative mindsets can you assume when you see these patterns arising in the future?
- What matters more to you than praise (Mohr, 2015)? How does tapping into your purpose, service, and contribution shift how you might receive feedback?

most cited piece of her career. It would have been easy to have accepted the shock of the first review as a message that her work wasn't valid.

Janelle was able to treat the process like the game that it is, and thankfully she had success the second time. No one is fully immune to the review process, however. If she had gotten a second rejection, she might have let the demons of the inner critics flow in like Harry Potter's Death Eaters.

In addition to the volleying analogy, the literature speaks of publishing as fishing versus baseball (James, 2014, p. 51). Conversations would then often consist of "Did you catch anything?" and the response would be "Not yet." Publishing is not about a batting average. Persistence matters more than failure.

SPEAK YOUR TRUTH

Inner critics also can stop the speaking of truth in the personal sense of purpose in research. It is possible to fall back on citing others rather than establishing contribution and conceding the value of our own work. This hesitation can grow after a rough review process.

When getting stuck on ruminating on the work of others, reviewers can paralyze writers into thinking that they cannot possibly write anything as well. It might reinforce the inner critics that their work is unworthy. By flipping the process and focusing on the original claims of the work, the piece will be stronger and the critics will fade away.

Reggie was an LGBTQ graduate student of color struggling with depression so serious that he considered dropping out of his Ph.D. program. He had recently moved away from his university to join his partner after defending his proposal. His distance from his institution made it even harder to focus on his work, and it felt like everyone else was having much more success than he was. He was stuck.

I challenged Reggie to write every day to make progress on his work, but he was spinning his wheels because he couldn't seem to get past the literature review. He thought he had to get the literature chapter just right before he could start his own analyses.

The lure of the literature kept him stuck. He kept reading the work of others, and the more he read, the more he felt that he could never write as well as they did. He also felt that there had to be more literature that he was not covering, and he was under the presumption that he must show that he knew *all* the scholarship on his topic. The literature was stopping him from being successful. It was calling forth his inner critic and making him feel like he was working when he actually was making no progress on completing his dissertation at all.

I told Reggie to stop revising his literature review and instead get busy finding his own voice by writing up his own research. He had shown in the proposal that he understood the relationship of his work to the broader field. He felt immediate relief when he learned that he could step away from the work of others and increase his sense of agency by focusing on what he could control—his own data collection, analysis, and findings.

Choose sources wisely when possible. Decide why to include citations and gain clarity on the purpose they serve. Kamler and Thomson (2014) use the image of a dinner party. Do not invite everyone. Choose carefully. As the author, even the mightiest of scholars must receive permission to enter into the piece.

Begin paragraphs with your ideas. Support claims with data or the citations of others in the rest of the paragraph. Place your own ideas up front in a clear manner, uncluttered by the work of others. This idea may feel backward compared to previous training; younger scholars are taught that it is important to learn from the experts of a field. When writing original work, these so-called experts can help explain the significance of your work. But writing is about speaking your own voice—the work of other scholars is included as a way to contextualize your own work. Authorship means that citation of the work of others builds toward an argument of your own contribution in the writing.

Try to not quote directly but instead paraphrase. Every author has their own writing style and rhythms; these rhythms will not be the same as that of another scholar. Reading a quotation feels like a hard stop to a reader because everything—the cadence, the tone—is different. Give credit where credit is due, but try to paraphrase instead. People read an article to know what that author has to say—not to have a summary of others. Remember that to keep that inner critic at bay.

RECOMMENDATIONS FOR UNIVERSITIES

- Provide opportunities for faculty to share struggles as well as successes with one another.
- Make the publishing process more transparent by offering panels and mentoring from faculty experienced in peer review.
- Share the reviews that senior faculty have received over their career.
- Discuss how different faculty approach writing peer reviews—to show both the range in processes as well as the different valid and invalid reasons for how to tackle the task.

Part II

STRENGTHENING ACADEMIC IDENTITY

CHAPTER 4

Agency

This chapter focuses on building *agency*—the ability of an individual to exert power and to influence contexts (Mitra, 2004, p. 655; O'Meara & Terosky, 2010). Agency cultivates confidence and self-worth. It creates a sense of empowerment that can lead to changes in habits and even lead one to be brave enough to work to change institutions (Mitra & Serriere, 2012).

In academia, agency includes ways that faculty can construct their own learning and development processes, as well as feel that their work is making an impact (Neumann, Terosky, & Schell, 2006). Faculty are motivated by their intrinsic commitments to their work (Blackburn & Lawrence, 1995). Agency is critical in defining a meaningful career, including striking a preferred work/life balance, finding needed resources, and engaging in work that is valued. It can be impacted by political and social contexts. Issues of bias and resources influence how faculty perceive their agency within their work environment (O'Meara, Lounder, & Campbell, 2014; O'Meara & Terosky, 2010).

This chapter examines processes to tap into inner wisdom to articulate purpose and values that undergird how to live a fulfilled life. Deepening agency as an academic consists of tethering scholarship to a greater sense of purpose. Working on projects that align with a sense of purpose is most often energizing rather than depleting. Seeking ways to foster feelings of creativity, curiosity, and agency within work helps to find meaning and purpose in academic life (Fritz, Lam, & Spreitzer, 2011). Taking a longer view on any task to assess how a project connects to purpose and impact correlates with career fulfillment. Additionally, attention is given to *how* work is conducted and how to author a piece with a sense of agency, and therefore to improve the impact of the quality of the work completed.

TAPPING INTO A DEEPER PURPOSE

Tethering to purpose helps to build efficacy, which is the belief behind the agency. Building stores of efficacy (Bandura, 2000) strengthens confidence, self-worth, and the belief of being able to make an impact, whether contributing to society writ large or to a specific situation (Mitra & Serriere, 2012).

Connecting research and writing to purpose allows you to tap into inspiration that can increase energy. The concept of being in a "flow" (Nakamura & Csikszentmihalyi, 2014) is an example of this process. Flow is the feeling of being so absorbed in a task that time loses its hold, and the process seems to be driven by a deeper source.

Ana requested coaching because she was not publishing enough. She had deep writer's block, and it led to a negative performance review. A top journal had rejected her piece, saying that the topic was not relevant to the field. Ana's work questioned the premises of the predominant framework in her discipline. She critiqued the lack of inclusivity of the dominant narrative and offered an approach that embraced her own intersectionalities as a Black, female, Lesbian scholar. Untangling the threads of her experience, her article reflected what she viewed as her purpose—her meaningful work. The rejection led her to believe that her field doubted the value of her work.

I asked Ana, "If the field did not value your work, would it stop your work?" Rather than becoming more discouraged, Ana redoubled her faith in her work. Part of her purpose, she believed, was to shift the field to embrace a broader range of perspectives. Rejection, then, will be expected, but she could feel in her core that her work was valuable and that she had to find the strength to engage in her work from within. Future rejections would fuel her fire rather than extinguish it.

Keeping purpose and values visible can help to remind scholars of why the work is worth the effort. This process can help scholars make tough decisions about when work does not align with the dominant paradigms. Purpose and value clarity can serve as a rubric for discerning difficult career decisions. It can also provide a reason to choose writing first over other demands during a given day.

CHARGE BATTERIES; DON'T DRAIN THEM

Academia relies on the ability to write and research. Persistently. Endlessly. Even when the mood does not strike us. If writing and research are not energizing, the passion for the subject may have gotten lost along the way. Or perhaps it was never found. The quality of scholarship is impacted by the ability to keep vitality levels high.

Empirical research from psychology and organizational theory has focused on how mindset "charges our batteries"—and what drains them. Swenson (2014) describes this process as keeping a margin of energy to avoid overload. Resources equal power, including time, strength, and knowledge. The burdens on the system consist of work, relationships, and expectations. The margin is the amount of resources left after taking into account all of our loads—Resources – Loads = Margin. Energy is needed to take on unexpected stressors. Without a margin, overload can lead to burn-out, stress, anxiety, depression, and dysfunctional relationships.

LEARNING WHAT PURPOSE FEELS LIKE

Tapping into purpose should feel like an unending source of energy that fuels the work. An important step in finding purpose is to understand how it feels within the body. Mohr (2015, p. 66) describes this feeling as a concept called *yirah*—a feeling of taking up a larger space and energy than you have before—maybe even more than you feel that you "should" have. It is a building of something bigger than oneself. It should feel inspiring and expansive. It may even build nervous energy—an anticipation of the work ahead that is aligned with a deeper sense of knowing.

Contrast this anticipation with fear, which feels like a dreaded, heavy weight. Fear is discouraging, whereas *yirah* feels inspirational.

Tom came to me hoping to learn how to be more efficient. He had too many tasks to complete and wanted to find an extra hour in the day. He was terribly worried about not getting tenure, even though he had twice the number of publications of anyone else in his department. We worked through the short-term overwhelming pile of deadlines by prioritizing, saying no to optional activities, and working on putting full energy only into the most meaningful activities.

Six months later, his plate was overflowing again. His struggle was not time management. With further unraveling of the questions, we saw that Tom found comfort in taking on too much. He held fast to the belief that his worth was only measured by the amount of work that he was completing and the extent that he could show others that he was busy.

I talked with Tom about the need to move deeper than organizational processes and time management to addressing underlying fears. Tom asked for frameworks and ways to cognitively process his work life. But I pushed back that he would need to seek guidance from his heart and gut. He was experiencing a block that was preventing him from feeling worthy. Tom had inner work to do on making peace with a trauma from his past that was making him a slave to himself. He would always feel exhausted and overworked until he could find purpose from within.

Finding this larger, more open and fulfilling space can begin with curiosity. The text box explores a process of how to gain wisdom from within the body—the heart, the gut, the hands, and more.

EMBODIED TRUTHS

Write down three words that define how you want to *feel* about your work. They could include words such as *inspired, joyful, innovative, fulfilled, authentic, powerful, impactful, groundbreaking, challenging, brave,* and *integrative.*

Sit with your eyes closed. Picture these "being" words and take three deep breaths. Then ask yourself, "What work can I do that most aligns with these ways of being?"

This exercise can be used for broad questions or for a specific project. Channel your purpose into your work.

IDENTIFYING CORE VALUES

Clarifying core values can also deepen purpose. Although passion alone might not be enough to persist in a career, conscious alignment of career choices with values can improve job satisfaction (Herrera, 2020). Values create a scaffolding with which it is possible to move beyond smaller ups and downs of a career and keep focused on a longer-term vision of purpose. Without connection to values, it becomes possible to slip into dismay, disenchantment, aimlessness, and cynicism when work goes awry.

Values can be formed through experiences, influential people, family structures and culture, and even difficult times. Common values for academics include giving back, creativity, innovation, making a difference, order/control, and equity (Clark & Sousa, 2018). Values may change over time. They may even conflict with some of the expectations of academia.

Identifying values is not just stating them—it is living them. Aligning with values also helps to dispel notions of perfection. By paying attention to the passion within the work, scholars can define a sense of inner standards rather than external judgment. The gap between work and vision should feel inspiring and energizing rather than depleting (Salzberg & Thurman, 2014). This mindful work allows a calibration of the importance of self-improvement without the destructive inner critics.

Articulating values can help you plan your career for the short and the long term. Doing so will keep you tethered to your purpose. Figure 4.1 offers resources for identifying values.

PURPOSE AS CAREER-LONG TRAJECTORY

Consideration of career shifts and hitting the doldrums of mid-career can be a time of needing to reconnect into core values. Associate professors are the most unhappy of academics, national data show (Collaborative on

Figure 4.1. Resources for Choosing Values

1. *Revisit a rewarding moment of success.* Think back to rewarding moments in your life—a particular moment in time when you felt a huge energy hit and felt as if you were flowing in the stream of success . . . a time when you felt fully alive. When using this strategy, draw on your senses to bring you back to the exact moment—where you were, how your body felt, what the light looked like, who you were with. By describing and feeling the moment fully, you can distill the essence of what made that moment special. Then consider what values/beliefs/principles underlie the meaning of this experience for you.
2. *Choose from a list of values.* Choose the values that define you the most from the list of values in Appendix A. Many people are instead choosing a word for the year as a point of focus rather than a resolution. Words include *inspire, joy, shine, focus,* and *audacity.* Drawing on your resolutions/goals/words for the year can also help to flesh out values (Brown, 2018).
3. *Ask colleagues what is important about your work.* Invite your most trusted peers to consider what they value about your work. Reread peer reviews—not for the criticism but to pull out what they say about your strengths and what the purpose is of your work. Listen for positive comments from discussions at conferences for what they value in your papers (don't listen only for the criticism).
4. *Curate a list of your gifts.* Ask 10 people from across your life, "What three words best describe me?" Or an even braver approach is to pose that question on social media. Create a visual collage, like a word cloud, of the words shared with you.
5. *Journal about your values* (Brown, 2018; Clark & Sousa, 2012; Robison, 2013),
   What do I wish to accomplish?
       How do you define "meaning" in your work?
       What academic work inspires me and why?
   What does it feel like when I live my values?
       What drives me to do excellent work?
       How do I want to show up as a scholar?
       Why did I choose a career in academia?
       How do I express my values in my work?
   What are signs that I am not living in my values?
       What struggles do I have with my scholarship?
       When do I experience conflicting values within my scholarship?
   What does support look like?
       Who can champion me to help me to live my values?

Academic Careers in Higher Education, 2007; Mathews, 2014). Research indicates that the most successful mid-career faculty look to an inner sense of purpose as a stronger force for the development of their research agenda. Thriving mid-career faculty tap into "passionate thought." They find excitement and fulfillment through the focus of research and teaching (Neumann, 2009).

Upon Lynnette's final promotion to full professor, she took a step back from her focus on publishing, publishing, publishing. She looked at her field and found it lacking a diverse set of voices, spaces to engage in scholarship of critique, and a successful blending of practitioners with researchers.

Looking at the scholars in her field, she realized that she was now at the stage of her career when it was her job to lead this work. She was now one of the senior people who needed to hold space and build opportunities for others.

She spent the next 5 years taking steps to convene a diverse group of scholars focused on their shared work. In partnership with colleagues, she created a new journal, established an annual conference, and designed an online space to continue collaboration between meetings.

She also took the time to learn more about how to create inclusive spaces, through the inclusion and invitation of a broader array of scholars and practitioners. As well, she engaged senior scholars in conversations about how their power and privilege could be turned toward consciously opening spaces for opportunities for a more diverse set of voices in the field.

Success in stoking and preserving this passion includes committing to ongoing learning, just as Lynnette committed to learning more about inclusion and privilege. Neumann (2009) speaks of the need to create space with work goals and responsibilities for ongoing learning. This process includes building networks and communities, as well as pruning away work that does not align with one's inner purpose. Learning, Neumann's research suggests, includes not just deepening our knowledge of research, but also learning about how our research fits into a broader array of responsibilities.

Universities must consider how to stoke learning as a form of leadership, passion, and purpose for everyone—and especially mid-career faculty. This stoking includes space for questioning, critique, and advocacy. Leadership is not the same as producing, the research indicates, and therefore supporting learning requires a different skill set than publishing. Time is needed to build diverse leaders, even if publishing slows.

FINDING LEADERS AND MENTORS WITHIN

Working with visual messages taps into inner wisdom in a three-dimensional way. Tapping into such wisdom requires turning our focus away from your head and toward the gut and heart. When running workshops on accessing inner wisdom, I am always surprised by how readily clients can access their inner critics but how hesitant and doubtful they are about accessing inner leaders. It feels more acceptable to identify critics than champions. The habit of accessing saboteurs is much more strongly formed than the habit of seeking positive sources of energy and light.

Display images of inspiration. Collect words and images that inspire a re-connection to purpose. Images might include a picture of one's grandmother who never had the chance to go to college, or a printed quotation from a favorite writer. Maya Angelou is famous for saying, "Your crown has already been paid for. Put it on your head and wear it."

Margot felt overwhelmed about the amount of chapters left to write in her thesis. She broke the task into smaller parts, but even then, she knew that she still had to write on days when her inspiration was not flowing because she was on a deadline. She wanted to do good-quality work, and she needed to stay focused.

Her inner critic kept creeping in, telling her that she was not writing in a technical manner. That she was not smart enough. That she would not get it done.

I asked her why she had chosen her topic. She had chosen to investigate the way the policy system is fragmented. She came to the topic after learning about the life of Elorie, a child Margot had tutored during graduate school. Elorie had been placed in foster care during those years, and Margot struggled to find her as she was transferred from home to home. Margot's description of this story reminded her of why she was researching policy processes.

I suggested that she keep a photo of Elorie taped to her computer for the remainder of her writing project. When she did not feel like writing, she could look at Elorie and find renewed inspiration to tackle her project.

Consider what images might inspire leadership and inner purpose. Think about how to channel determination and focus into one's work help to carry on that legacy. Others like to post photos of themselves when they were strong, bold, even sassy. Photos of "3-year-old you" in a cowboy hat? The photo of winning the high school championship? Called "inner children" in coaching literature, all of those brave souls are still within and can be channeled.

Work with guided visualization to identify an inner leader. I learned about the inner leader process during my training with the Coaches Training Institute (Kimsey-House, Kimsey-House, Sandahl, & Whitworth, 2018), and ever since I have included inner leader processes in all of the workshops that I run across the country. Central to this process is tapping into the inner wisdom within us that can guide us to align our work to our own life's purpose. Guided imagery is one way to tap into this inner wisdom. Often the inspiration from these exercises is surprising, offering new ways of seeing. These visions can provide creative solutions and additional ways of viewing life rather than making a hard choice between two options. They help to pull a camera into a wide-angle perspective on life—away from a too-close-up view of an immediate problem.

The following text box offers two guided visualizations for finding inspiration from within. Success with these exercises requires moving past discomfort with visualization to embrace the positive forces that provide ongoing support. "Bravery," according to Brown (2018), is choosing courage over comfort.

Supporting oneself can feel courageous. The choice to access inner wisdom is like learning to flex a new muscle. It takes practice as well as faith that it is in there. It might feel clumsy at first. But with practice, you can choose to draw on the positive sources from within instead of the negative. It can also feel fun and joyful to find inner strength.

Lean into the playful aspect of the exercises in the text box, but with one note of caution—a survivor of deep trauma might find visualization frightening because it requires trusting the inner landscape. If visualization feels unsafe at a core level, find a certified helping professional to assist with the process of letting go of embedded fear and grief. The work is even more important if resistance arises; resistance signals an opportunity to move through stuck places and to begin healing. But that does not mean this work should be done alone. Find support as needed to engage in this work if it is tapping into hidden wells of fear.

Diana came to me knowing that she wanted to quit her job as a project manager of a nonprofit focused on homelessness but did not have a sense of what she wanted to do with her life instead. She had always had a passion for homelessness issues but could not understand why she was miserable in her current job. In fact, she was finally compelled to find a coach after attending a weekend retreat in which a walk in the woods caused her to repeat endlessly in her head, "I hate my job."

Diana was baffled by this message, because she had wanted to work on homelessness issues since attending college. Using her mind to logically think through her career was getting her stuck. Her inner critic flared.

I guided Diana through the future visualization so she could tap into her inner wisdom to help discern her career path. In the visualization, Diana saw her future self living high up on a mountainside, with a view of a foggy valley below. She had a loyal dog at her side. Sheep grazed at a distance. Her cottage was filled with books she had written, writing materials for future projects, and art from her travels around the world.

The future self offered Diana tea. She conveyed a sense of comfort, contentment, and a life well lived. She exuded serenity and perspective. She was a mentor to others and had created a space that served as an inspiration.

Coming out of the visualization, Diana noted that the predominant feeling she received was the identity of herself as a writer. Her current job focused on event planning, and she had lost the opportunity to share her voice through writing projects. She wanted to stay in her current field but was going to either find a way to shift her current job responsibilities to include time for

TOOLS FOR FINDING THE INNER LEADER

Sit very still. Close your eyes. Take deep breaths. Place your concentration on your belly as you breathe in and out. Take five deep breaths, allowing a pause after each inhale and exhale. When you find your body relaxing and your mind clearing, follow these steps:

1. **Imagine your inner leader.** Ask yourself what image would embody you at your strongest. Sit down in a safe place with this leader and ask these questions, allowing plenty of time between them: *What do I need to know? How can you support me? What gifts do you offer me?* Research the meaning behind the names and images that arise to find greater insight. Create visual images of your inner source of strength. Keep these images visible to help you to tap into your strength. Examples of inner leaders from my clients include warriors, gods and goddesses, a sacred elder, a lion, an oak tree, Hercules with a large sword, a phoenix, and even a crusty sea captain. Engage in this exercise from a place of curiosity and even playfulness.

    No single image must be the correct one. In fact, it is possible to have not only one inner leader but a team of support. My inner leaders include an Indian warrior goddess, a playful Tinkerbell spirit, and a sacred grandmother. Each provides a different type of energy that I can draw upon, depending on the work I am doing, the people I am encountering, and the ways in which I wish to show up in that moment. My inner warrior goddess helps me to persist in the final stages of writing a book when I am tired and my energy is failing. I channel the vision of a sacred grandmother during a difficult conversation with my teenage daughter. I call upon Tinkerbell when I have been working too hard and need to find playful joy in my life.

2. **Ask your future self.** Picture in your mind your future self. Begin by imagining where in the world your future self lives. Look at the structure where your future self lives. Take yourself to the front door. Enter the dwelling. Greet your future self. Sit down with a cup of your favorite beverage and ask these questions, allowing plenty of time between them: *What do I need to know to get from now until where you are? What matters most in these upcoming years? What advice do you have for me?*

Note: Both of these visualizations are commonly used in coaching. Many audio versions exist of each of these meditations online. Sitting with eyes closed in a quiet space, perhaps with a journal nearby, is a recommended process for this work.

writing projects or look for other positions in which she could have a greater amount of her time fitting with her need to write.

Diana's future self was an intersection of her values and beliefs. Her purpose aligned with writing and mentoring others. She brought nature into her space and had easy access to nature just outside her door. Diana could see the alignment of her career's purpose and her values in this house and this wise older woman.

Once these images emerge, they offer a great tool for discernment of tough decisions, of prioritizing work, and of aligning inner selves with work goals and expectations. When in doubt, ask what that inner leader or future self might do in a situation. Consider designing workspace to reflect how an inner mentor might work. Think about how an inner mentor might dress, speak, teach, and write.

RECOMMENDATIONS FOR UNIVERSITIES

- Invest in opportunities for continuous learning for faculty across the faculty lifespan—including learning how to teach, write, and lead.
- Foster opportunities to build relationships among faculty to encourage technical collaboration as well as emotional support, never underestimating the power of food and fellowship to encourage gathering together.
- Encourage opportunities to connect faculty to their purpose for their work. Feedback and performance reviews can offer these opportunities as well as training for department heads and related leaders in how to support faculty.

CHAPTER 5

Research

Most academics at research institutions have an expectation of research built into their time. For example, they might have 50% of their time expected to be focused on research and 50% focused on teaching and service. They might teach two courses a semester. Keeping a research focus in any context is challenging—even more so for faculty who may want to find a future position at a research-focused institution but are currently teaching four to five courses per semester.

Research on faculty development indicates that the expectations for research productivity also are dramatically increasing post-tenure and promotion as well (Philipsen & Bostic, 2010). This pressure to produce work, plus the freedom to work "anywhere" through the help of technology, can also lead us to never feel that work is hard to "turn off." Colbeck and Wharton-Michael (2006) describe this shift in working environment plus added expectations as giving faculty "the freedom to work themselves to death" (p. 47).

The content of research varies dramatically for faculty. It can mean traditional experiments in "bench" sciences, to composing operas, to surveying high school students. The common thread across academic research is the need to excel at completing good-quality work and publishing it.

BUILDING A SCHOLARLY IDENTITY

Identifying one's scholarly identity, including one's contribution to research, is central to success in research-focused academic positions. This identity and impact influences the ability to acquire funding, to write persuasively, and to get published.

Aligning values and research agenda strengthens the process of developing (or revising) a scholarly identity. Stronger stores of agency can lead to a better articulation of purpose and of how work can be impactful and significant. This articulation can be important during promotion and tenure processes, job searches, and even grant applications. The text box offers ways to picture your academic audiences and consider how you would describe your work in ideal terms.

SHARPENING YOUR RESEARCH IDENTITY

- If you were in the elevator with the president of your university or your research association and had 30 seconds to be memorable and describe your research, what would you say?
- Your future self receives a lifetime achievement award. What would the person introducing you say about the scope of your work and your contribution?
- You have been given a chance to tweet on the biggest platform in your field. What would you say?

Building a scholarly identity is the academic version of building a brand. This language may sound crass or awkward to academics. "I'm not in the job to make a buck," an academic might claim. Often scholars feel that research should speak for itself. Women, in particular, tend to be reluctant self-promoters, since research that shows that women can incur social costs and are seen as less likable when self-advocating (Mohr, 2015, p. 134). Yet the reality is that self-promotion is necessary to introduce work to others and to find ways that work intersects with others and with research fields.

Defining a scholarly brand includes defining your contribution. This process is manifested in a promotion narrative, a biography, and a personal website. The product needs to have a core thread to it that allows work to be understood and identifiable. Continuing to hone the message and to tie it more deeply to your purpose can help you decide which projects to choose, which papers to write, and how to articulate the value of your work.

Keeping these audiences in mind can help you create an outward-facing process to design and share your work. This stance can help you craft research design and publication writing to have a greater focus on the significance of the work beyond the immediate research and the implications of the work for others. Connecting your brand to your values and purpose can also help to deepen the connection to broader causes and future opportunities.

Work on a two-sentence version of a purpose statement. Use this short version to keep visible the reason behind the work. Writing a clear message will also help you prioritize research, teaching, and service. Every assignment accepted and choice made should fit within this purpose statement.

Keep key words consistent. Building a brand includes being searchable on social media. When you are building expertise within a research area, a goal should include being one of the first author names listed when searching that area of scholarship. For all publications written, keep terms consistent so that your full body of work can be easily found. Having your name recognizable is part of building a brand.

When I started my research, for example, the brand of "student voice" was thin in the literature on educational change. I have included these words in most titles and every abstract of my writing since my dissertation. Twenty years later, I am one of the first hits that comes up on Google searches for the concept. A consistency of concept means that my work can be found easily. The titles of my work also provide a clear line on which to build my narrative statement when preparing for promotions.

Build a scholarly social media presence. The use of social media outlets is becoming an expected part of how to share your work as an academic. As a scholar, you need to share news efficiently, but do not let this goal carve into time that could be used for writing for publication. Beyond sharing your work with others, think of how to build connections by sharing news about colleagues as well and building relationships in which cross-promotion can occur. Beware, however, of the trap of spending too much time on social media. Endless tweeting or writing for social media outlets can be time better spent on writing for peer review. Too much self-promoting can be criticized in promotion processes.

MAXIMIZING PUBLISHING WHILE PROTECTING PURPOSE

For early-career academics, it is important to learn the promotion rules of their institution, department, and field of study. It is also important to maintain an awareness of the standards more broadly in case the need or choice to move to another university arises. Some academic departments will expect solo publications; others are mainly looking for first-authored pieces as a sign of strong scholarship. Some tenure and promotion processes also will encourage collaboration with students. Knowing these expectations can help you when mapping out your publication plans.

It is important to have a clear and long-term strategy of maximizing publication. Many fields prioritize the importance of peer-reviewed journals. Some value published conference proceedings. Other fields instead prefer a book. In my field, a book counts for about the same amount as an article but takes many times the effort. A book can therefore be the "icing on the cake" of the dossier for a pre-tenured faculty member, but if a book is written and the number of articles seems slim, that could cause trouble in the promotion process. Ask questions regarding books versus articles for each field to understand the expectations.

For most academic fields, solicited book chapters do not get much respect because they do not undergo peer review. You should never publish your best work in a book chapter, and maybe not even spend time on book chapters at all. The exception is any opportunity to position yourself as an expert, such as writing a chapter in a prestigious handbook that includes all the top scholars in a field.

Consideration of where to send scholarship should begin when you are constructing the piece. Writing for an audience is critical for acceptance. Instead of targeting one publication as a goal, consider a cluster of two to three targets. Think about whether the publishing venue would require an asterisk—an explanation to stave off a concern in a performance review. Only choose "asterisks" if they align with your purpose and values or if they serve a political goal. Otherwise, publish in peer-reviewed, high-quality outlets.

When I was a graduate student, I attended a panel of Stanford University professors who were giving advice on strategies for developing a publishing strategy. I heard two very different but complementary perspectives on how to approach publishing.

First, an older, White male scholar stood up and hammered home the importance of tiers of journals. The type of professor who appears intimidating at first but who underneath is a big champion for students, he began his talk by standing up and pacing. Fully fitting the character, he spoke with a gruff voice and kept adjusting his belt as he walked back and forth in front of the audience.

"Know the hierarchy of the journals," he barked out. "Start at the top and make your way down the hierarchy in terms of priorities of publication. Create a sequence of journals in which an article could fit, beginning with the top-tier journal, then a field-specific journal, then a journal that is likely to publish most work. Or choose another journal of the same tier if a rejection was due to fit with that journal and not a critique of the quality of the piece."

A second professor spoke on the panel—a female, White, pre-tenured scholar. She was soft-spoken and careful with her word choice. She stressed the process of choosing the conversations you wanted to have and focused on the alignment between your contribution and the focus of the journal— that is, align your purpose with your scholarship. She suggested looking at the editorial board—the more names you recognize (and even better, people you cite often), the greater the likelihood that this journal might be a fit.

I use this model of journal tiers regularly in my teaching on academic writing because I love the juxtaposition of the gruff focus on the competition

Figure 5.1. Journal Tiers

Top tier: Journals speaking to the breadth of a field (such as education or sociology); often they are affiliated with the top research association of a field
Second tier: Top journals in a subfield (such as educational leadership or demography)
Third tier: Lesser-known journals in a subfield (narrower subfields and journals with lower reputations)

with the emphasis on conversation (see Figure 5.1). Both matter. The first part is learning how to play the game of academia. The second is keeping purpose central while playing the game. Owning voice and choice in decisions—that is the agency present to navigate the space between structure and self while developing an academic persona.

WHEN PURPOSE QUESTIONS DOMINANT PARADIGMS

Faculty can face discrimination within the academy when designing research that differs from dominant paradigms (Rockquemore, 2015). Institutional policies and individuals in power using dominant paradigms may privilege certain forms of research over others and keep the scope of what is considered "rigorous" to a very narrow band of scholarship (Griffin et al., 2011).

In recent research on what qualities future leaders need most, a unanimous response is courage and bravery (Brown, 2015). Leaders need the courage to engage in difficult conversations and the bravery to assert the need for new ways of seeing. Bravery in scholarship can include questioning newer methodologies, valuing a broader range of voices as legitimate, questioning premises as biased, and bringing in the experiences of individuals as data.

New scholarship should question the boundaries of disciplines. Scholars must have the agency to make strategic choices about how and when to present ideas that challenge dominant paradigms. Draw on the lessons from previous chapters and know the unspoken rules of institutions and the field when deciding whether to assert your purpose and perspective.

Deciding what to publish and when requires connecting to your purpose and values. Some scholarship can wait until after tenure, whereas other scholarship is central to your identity, purpose, and goals. You must make personal choices based on risk, larger work/life balance issues, and personal values regarding the claims and arguments you feel are needed and at what time. Gaining information about potential consequences of holding your ground is critical. Talk to trusted friends and colleagues to weigh your options. Know what conditions at your university are so toxic or problematic that they are worth changing jobs or careers to maintain the agency of your path and purpose.

Brandon's research examined issues "on the diagonal"—a term I use to explain when a scholar draws upon ideas from multiple disciplines to form a new look at a body of scholarship. His work combined concepts from psychology and mathematics to draw attention to issues of bias and discrimination within these fields.

Sometimes Brandon's work would be rejected without being sent out for review due to "fit." He published prolifically but often in lower-tier journals because the main journals of psychology and of mathematics teaching did not have much interest in this joint type of scholarship.

I worked with Brandon to focus on the introduction and discussion sections of his paper to articulate why this "diagonal" form of research should be valuable for each of the disciplines at the heart of his work. Compared to other scholars, he had to take extra space and care to explain the legitimacy of his work. He needed to use creativity and his passion to show the contribution of his original work at connecting the two fields.

When it came time for tenure, Brandon painstakingly crafted his narrative statement to define his impact as an academic. He articulated the significance of his scholarship, explained his choice of journals, aligned them to his contribution, and showed his trajectory of research and goals for his scholarship moving forward. He sought out external reviewers who spoke to the value of his scholarship and the impact he was making while choosing a tougher pathway through the publication process. Brandon learned that he received tenure based on his ability as well as the ability of his external reviewers to articulate the connection between his purpose and his choices of how he designed his scholarship.

Research agendas that question the status quo can be considered controversial and judged as lacking rigor because the definition of quality is not aligned with the dominant paradigm (Griffin et al., 2011; Lewis & Simpson, 2012; Louis, 2007; Rockquemore & Laszloffy, 2008). Often, underrepresented scholars face a dilemma of choosing between conducting research that aligns with their lived experiences and conducting scholarship within the confines of what the academy has deemed as "acceptable" and "rigorous." By designing work that is different, faculty faces a greater risk of delegitimization and denouncement.

It is critical for institutions, and the individuals within them who are in power, to call out narrow definitions of scholarship and to make space for a broader approach to valuing scholars' different ways of knowing. Indeed, finding ways to value taking risks in scholarship stretches our fields in exciting directions—for tenure, for new positions, and for defining lifelong careers. This stretching of disciplines and being inclusive of new scholarship should be the responsibility of the institution and of senior scholars.

RECOMMENDATIONS FOR UNIVERSITIES

- Value and reward equity-focused research—and especially research that may not be eligible for external funding.
- Offer a junior sabbatical option—a semester off midway through the tenure track that allows junior faculty to dive deeper into a research agenda.
- Incentivize the development of writing groups and research collaboration for faculty and for graduate students.
- Entice community and collaboration through the creation of rituals—seminars, coffee hours, celebrations. Include small offerings of food and drink at such events.
- Encourage interdisciplinary collaboration across units that can lead to the development of external funding.
- Value a broader range of ways that academics can make a contribution to society, often called "public scholarship." Encourage creativity of contribution.
- Provide transparent and clear conflict-of-interest rules and processes that encourage innovation and entrepreneurship.

CHAPTER 6

Belonging

Chronic loneliness is proving to be an epidemic of present-day society (Cacioppo & Patrick, 2008), with more than 40% of the U.S. population reporting loneliness even before the pandemic changed all of our lives forever (Entis, 2016). Building connection to others aligns with life satisfaction, well-being, and purpose. Citing the research of Cacioppo and Cacioppo (2017), Brown (2017) states, "To grow as an adult is not to become autonomous and solitary—but to become the one on whom others can depend" (p. 25).

With the onset of the COVID-19 pandemic, discussions of isolation and loneliness became omnipresent. With the knowledge that academic work will be forever changed post-pandemic, no one knows just how working remotely will become a more permanent part of academia. Even before the pandemic, however, scholars experienced loneliness within universities. The culture of some departments has always been one of closed doors or working away from the office.

This growing epidemic of loneliness is layered onto institutional racism that has intentionally caused minoritized faculty and students to feel disconnected from academic institutions. This disconnection can stem from culture, gender, ethnicity, or sexual orientation, among other intersectionalities. These disconnections can lead to exclusion from networks and a lack of invitation to social activities and informal spaces (Rockquemore & Laszloffy, 2008; Turner, González, & Wong, 2011). Griffin's review (2020) documents research showing that faculty identifying as women and as people of color are less likely to be satisfied with coworkers and report being treated unfairly and left out of social interactions (Bilimoria, Joy, & Liang, 2008; Seifert & Umbach, 2008).

This chapter examines the types of belonging needed in academic settings. Although it focuses on individual faculty needs, the expectation should be that universities design and promote structures that support inclusive belonging. Universities should be proactive in encouraging and supporting collaborations across departmental and traditional boundaries. They should especially seek out collaborative opportunities for underrepresented faculty and students.

CONNECTING TO OTHERS

I define *belonging* as connecting to others and relating to a broader context (Mitra, 2004). Sometimes called "relatedness" in the literature (Deci & Ryan, 2000; Osher, Cantor, Berg, Steyer, & Rose; 2020; Scales, Benson, & Roehlkepartain, 2011), belonging consists of opportunities to learn with and from others (Costello, Toles, Spielberger, & Wynn, 2000; Goodenow, 1993; Programme for Internal Student Assessment [PISA], 2003; Roeser et al., 1996). A sense of belonging is positively related to motivation (Goodenow, 1993; Ryan & Powelson, 1991), which can help with writing productivity and job satisfaction.

Belonging in academia has tended to be about expecting diverse faculty to fit into the university paradigm. Institutions instead must emphasize belonging structures that do not require assimilation into a dominant paradigm. Such activities would increase positive energy through respectful engagement, building trust, generating identities that connect to one's purpose and worth, and opportunities for growth and development (Dutton, 2003; Dutton & Heaphy, 2003; Quinn, 2007). These activities provide processes that reenergize people in the workplace focused on activities that build belonging and increased vitality—and especially activities that focus on showing gratitude toward colleagues and building connections between them (Fritz, Lam, & Spreitzer, 2011). Research on college student belonging connects this concept to perceived social support and feeling connected to others (Strayhorn, 2018, p. 3).

Belonging, therefore, should not mean blending in or sacrificing a core sense of self. Instead, it should focus on an institutional effort to redefine structures to facilitate belonging. Faculty motivation and job satisfaction correlate with the quality of relationships with colleagues and students (O'Meara et al., 2008) and to the ability to create meaningful social connections and build structures that support these connections (Collins, 2004; Quinn, Spreitzer, & Lam, 2012). Specifically, building relationships that are collaborative, nonhierarchical, and cross-cultural can improve the culture of the university as well as improve our well-being (Sorcinelli & Yun, 2007). Generation X faculty, for example, tend to seek out flatter organizational structures (Bova & Kroth, 2001). These flatter types of structures require stronger ties among colleagues and allow for ongoing feedback and learning opportunities.

The extent of collegial relations has been related to job satisfaction for pre-tenure women (August & Waltman, 2004). Others experience loneliness by accepting the only job offer in an isolated part of the country far away from family and friends. The onus therefore should be on universities to take institutional responsibility to invest in cultural changes that allow for a broader group of faculty (and students and staff) to see themselves reflected in the university culture and structures.

The need for belonging and connection continues through a faculty career. Being an associate professor has been described as "isolating and overwhelming" (Blanchard, 2012; Wilson, 2012) due to a lack of guidance for designing a career once tenure and promotion have been granted. Mid-career academic identities become challenged again due to the repetition of the same job without potential for further advancement.

Faculty benefit from building connections, including processes and activities focused on showing gratitude to colleagues (Quinn, Spreitzer, & Lam, 2012). The remainder of this chapter details the types of communities needed for academics. It includes finding collaborators who can create intellectual connection. The chapter then considers how to create support spaces by seeking out mentors and support spaces.

INTELLECTUAL SPACES: FINDING COLLABORATORS

This chapter focuses on the types of connections that faculty need to be successful, while stressing that the responsibility for creating such spaces must fall on universities if they claim to support diversity, equity, and inclusion. Successful faculty must be able to find opportunities to join and build intellectual communities. Scholarly collaboration can boost creativity, motivation, and clarity of scholarship (Fries-Britt & Kelly, 2005). Extensive research points to the importance of social networks of colleagues who share information (Uzzi, 2019). Connecting to multiple networks is preferred to one source of relatedness.

Faculty experience greater well-being, fulfillment, and success when they have established successful collaborations with colleagues. Although some research indicates that belonging comes before communities (Strayhorn, 2012), finding community spaces can also create opportunities for repairing or increasing belonging. Research from education and business refers to this type of belonging as a *community of practice*—a space to come together to deepen their understanding of a common problem by interacting on an ongoing basis (Mitra, 2008). Participation in communities of practice can increase productivity, well-being, and satisfaction by enabling scholars to interact with one another, share insights, and build a collective knowledge base (Wenger, McDermott, & Snyder, 2002). Stronger ties and co-research can lead to greater social capital, rewards, and recognition (Butner, Burley, & Marbley, 2000; Exum, Menges, Watkins, & Berglund, 1984; Griffin et al., 2011) as well as build rapport and positive assessments by colleagues (Stanley, 2006). Positive relationships with colleagues can even help reduce inequities experienced in university promotion practices (Drennan, Clarke, Hyde, & Politis, 2013; Rockquemore & Laszloffy, 2008).

The ability to find colleagues in other places in a university could open up opportunities to make use of incentive funds for interdisciplinary collaboration. Having a collaborator from another discipline can lead to publishing opportunities in a new set of journals and conferences to speak about the intersection of fields.

Underrepresented faculty may struggle with brokering such relationships due to institutional expectations that align with dominant paradigms. Relationships, therefore, often need to include an assessment of the extent to which colleagues and leaders are strategic allies who are willing to bridge and broker opportunities.

Finding collaborators within a department might be ideal for some. Research indicates that stronger ties and co-research within the department especially can lead to greater social capital, rewards, and recognition (Butner et al., 2000; Exum et al., 1984; Griffin et al., 2011) as well as build rapport and positive assessments by colleagues (Stanley, 2006). In contrast, a lack of collaboration within a department might cause less interaction with department faculty, and that can lead to more negative assessments or a perceived lack of fit with the department (Exum et al., 1984).

As a new professor, my research on student voice in school reform did not have a natural fit with other professors in my Department of Education Policy in the College of Education. Indeed, this problem can often be the reason that departments seek to diversify their course offerings, and therefore, many faculty members do not have much overlap in research interests in their immediate programs. I came to learn, however, that scholars were conducting similar work in related fields across my university. I found scholars interested in youth development outcomes in the College of Health and Human Development. I even found faculty conducting very similar work in the College of Agriculture—doing work on youth-adult partnerships in afterschool programs. I also found collaborators in the College of Liberal Arts rhetoric program focused on democracy.

You might have to creatively seek out collaborators, even within your own institution. Think creatively about where synergistic work might be happening. The best collaborators might also be on the other side of the world. The best collaborations also might be more about work patterns, such as the pace of the writing process. They might also center more around the values of scholarship rather than the particular focus of a project.

MULTIPLE SOURCES OF SUPPORT

I suggest that academics need colleagues of many kinds, stemming from research, teaching, and service relationships. It is important to have access to knowledge and support from multiple sources.

Research partners. Find colleagues aligned with your values and purpose to help create a sense of belonging on campus—and especially for professional advancement on campus and elsewhere.

Field-related collaborators. At national conferences and within universities, establish relationships with other people in your organizational field/topic. These peers may be in other sectors, such as practitioners, government officials, and research funders. These relationships can help you keep abreast of current research and can turn into potential collaborations down the road.

Institutional peers. Colleagues can help with benchmarking expectations and career progress, as well as trading information on the similarities and differences of unspoken rules in your field. Watch out for comparison and imposter syndrome; walk the fine line between gathering information to forward your own career path and the ways that the inner critic might spark jealousy instead of strength.

Service collaborators. Collaboration through service can find like-minded people with common goals for values, such as ethics, equity, and access. Such work also can increase institutional knowledge and add information about breaking the academic code, including understanding budgets, meeting senior leadership, and identifying new potential collaborators (Bird, 2011; O'Meara, Kuvaeva, et al., 2017).

Writing groups. Writing groups and partners can create a collaborative process. Extra sets of eyes from your discipline as well as from other backgrounds can boost the quality of your scholarship and productivity.

BUILDING A COMMUNITY

The onus should be on institutions to expand their notions of community to prioritize the inclusion and support of underrepresented faculty. Research indicates that faculty of color report low levels of satisfaction in building personal relationships with tenured colleagues and few opportunities for collaboration with tenured faculty (Collaborative on Academic Careers in Higher Education, 2007). Since universities also tend to be in White, upperclass areas, much has been written about the isolation from community that can be especially true for faculty of color, who find it challenging to locate spiritual, emotional, and social communities near their places of work (Griffin et al., 2011). Underrepresented faculty need to find community within their own identities, and they must often build their own support structures since they are nonexistent in current institutions. Such actions can promote persistence among underrepresented faculty by affirming identities, building trust, and maintaining faculty motivation (Fries-Britt & Snider, 2015; Garrison-Wade et al., 2012; Griffin, 2020; Kelly & Winkle-Wagner, 2017).

At a rural White college town in Pennsylvania, faculty of color assistant professors created the Docta Sistas—faculty from a broad range of disciplines. A group that has persisted for over 12 years, it has been the source of multiple writing groups. It also offers social opportunities for members, including salsa dancing and running half-marathons together. It provides a space for confidential conversations and advice. It offers a space for feedback when preparing dossiers and for providing advice on who in the university is supportive when debating how to address microaggressions and discriminatory colleagues.

Research indicates the importance of close contacts with other under-represented faculty to share private information about support and constraints for faculty advancement for these groups (Uzzi, 2019). Intentionally creating communities of support for underrepresented faculty can provide a sense of connection as well as a safe place to ask questions about the unspoken code of the university.

For universities lacking an affinity group such as Docta Sistas, finding kindred spirits in a large university can be challenging. Research indicates that service activities can be one way for underrepresented faculty to build a network of support on campuses that otherwise feel isolated and alienating (Baez, 2000; Griffin et al., 2013; Stanley, 2006), although they can also be an extra burden of responsibility (see the next chapter for an extended discussion of this dilemma). Individuals might also want to try to build their own support groups, either in person or virtually across university contexts.

COLLABORATIONS GONE AWRY

When the fit is not strong between scholars, collaboration can increase workload. This stress can focus on authorship and work styles or extend to microaggressions and bias. When politically delicate struggles start to emerge in a collaboration, the faculty and students with the least power often struggle to find a way out of the collaboration. The energy required to sustain these faulty collaborations can suck up the energy needed for faculty members' own writing and research.

Elena was a pre-tenured faculty member focused on publishing. She faced the misfortune of having two important manuscripts in her pipeline stall due to collaborators not completing their tasks. One collaborator was a senior faculty member who had asked Elena to work on a project. The second collaborator was a pre-tenured faculty member at another university who had subsequently chosen to leave academia for a research think tank.

Elena felt stuck and had to keep her writing moving. In both cases, the other author did not have the incentive to work as quickly as needed for Elena. For the senior faculty member, Elena felt she had to say yes to the collaboration despite having reservations. For the colleague who left the tenure track, Elena was faced with changing circumstances after the process had begun.

I worked with Elena on how to improve her communication with her collaborators. She offered to take greater responsibility for the workload to ensure that the pieces would keep moving forward. She kept her tone persistent and firm, but pleasant. She ended up spending more time on these pieces for only partial credit than she had intended. But with her leadership, both pieces were published within the year. Elena has learned from the experience that she will not be working with either of these colleagues again on a writing project.

Collaborations may not end up as one hopes, especially if it is the first time working with someone. Elena was wise to begin both of these collaborations, but she was frustrated to find a lack of shared urgency with her writing partners.

It is always helpful to speak about authorship and order of authorship explicitly before beginning collaborations. Create an ongoing expectation of keeping work moving forward. When stuck in unproductive collaborations, nudge colleagues gently but persistently. Elena was wise to politely keep nudging and remind her colleagues of her tight timeline toward tenure. Eventually both publications came through, but with a great deal of extra concern.

What mattered most was Elena's resolve to not collaborate with these specific colleagues again. Too many times, clients express grave concerns about a joint project, but then say yes again when the colleague suggests another opportunity for collaboration. As Maya Angelou once said, "When someone shows you who they are, believe them the first time."

When planning a pipeline of research productivity (discussed in Chapter 8, "Competencies"), consider new collaborations as bonus publications, since the timeline is not fully under your control. Having timeline conversations up front can also be a useful strategy, giving you the opportunity to explain pre-tenure pressures and determine whether the collaboration is timely or should wait until after other publications are submitted.

STRATEGIC CONFERENCING

Academics are often comfortable with letting their research and publications speak for themselves. Yet networking is essential, and the process can take time. Having a stronger network can help academics find everything from a research collaborator to a new job. It is best to view networking as a planting of seeds, slowly over time. The benefit of these seeds blooms over the course of a career.

Getting known by others can lead to invitations for collaboration on research and publication opportunities. Many strategies related to networking and conferencing can build relationships that can strengthen one's academic identity and well-being.

Identify key people. Investigate colleagues by exploring their webpages and online presence. Learn what conferences they attend and what professional societies they choose to join. Make introductions to others at the conferences by complimenting their work in specific terms. Invite them to serve as discussants on conference panels.

Strategically choose conferences where you can meet others and be known. Academics are expected to have a national reputation, and eventually an international reputation. Part of this reputation-building includes consistent presentations at top conferences. In addition to the very large meetings, consider presenting at smaller conferences, where it might be easier to meet people and to build connections. Be creative as to where these spaces might be. For example, my research was of interest to scholars who studied ethics, teacher leadership, and civic engagement—fields that I had not identified as my own. Attending meetings on these other topics allowed me to publish in a broader range of journals once I understood how my scholarship might be useful theoretically to those fields.

Plan ahead with networking strategies at conferences. At larger conferences, it may not be possible to meet people unless you have devised a strategy for networking. Decide ahead of time which key individuals you want to meet and others you want to reconnect with. Attend the receptions. Walk up and down the main corridors with the intention of meeting people rather than solely getting from one session to another.

Find collaborators through national service opportunities at conferences. Agreeing to serve on national committees is another way to build relationships that can lead to future opportunities. Seek out introductions that can build toward leadership positions at the national and international levels. Find smaller communities within the larger conferences. Attend the business meetings of divisions and special interest groups (SIGS). Learn the organizational structures and who to ask to become involved. Volunteer to be a part of these organizations as early as possible.

Talk to journal editors. If you are unsure what conversations to join, one way to learn more is to talk to journal editors. Major conferences often have journal editors available to answer questions at some point during the meeting.

Avoid trying to pitch an idea in much detail and asking if it would get published. They cannot possibly know from one conversation. Attend with the intention of learning about the journal and the editor. Ask about the scope of the journal, the type of pieces published, and what they are *not* looking for as much as what they are. Learn whether the journal publishes only empirical work or theoretical contributions. Send conceptual, passion pieces to quicker publication outlets or save them for book chapters.

Shop for a book contract. Unlike journal submissions, a book proposal should be sent to many publishing houses at one time—unless the publisher requests otherwise. If shopping for a book contract, timing that process around a major conference is a great idea.

Big meetings tend to have an exhibits hall. I thought the point of the publishers' hall was to sell books. It took me a while as an academic to learn that the editors from these presses attend these meetings to speak with potential authors about manuscripts.

I have found the face-to-face conversations with book editors to be much more substantive than sending proposals and trying to request a meeting. At a conference, they are a captive audience and are looking to fill their days talking to prospective authors. Even the editors who have not wanted to publish my work spend the time at conferences teaching me what they liked about the work and what they did not.

Again, as with a journal editor, pitching an idea at a meeting tends to be a thin way to have a conversation. It can be a way to learn about their press, much like a journal editor. With a book proposal, however, it is appropriate to provide the proposal beforehand, and therefore meetings at a conference can be extremely productive with book editors. I send my book proposals to a publisher about a month before the conference; I can then request meetings with many publishing houses during the conference.

Use current networks to meet new people. Build off networks—both current and former colleagues and mentors. Tag along to their receptions and ask them for introductions to others. Beyond conferences, ask colleagues from other universities for invitations to their university to give a talk and offer to do the same—in symposia or even by exchanging guest lectures at home universities. Such strategies can build mutual name recognition.

Covet participant lists. When a participant list is provided at a small meeting, spend time exploring the list. Look for commonalities. Make introductions at the meeting if possible or reach out via email later. Follow participants on social media, such as Twitter and LinkedIn, to learn more about their work and also to be able to find them in the future.

NETWORK EVERYWHERE

The hallways might be the most important spots in conferences. Talking to colleagues between scheduled sessions, or going up to scholars after presentations, can be more important than attending paper sessions. At one conference when I was pre-tenure, I was feeling crunched for time. I was facing many publishing deadlines and was up for a high-stakes annual review in a few months. During the meeting, I retired to my room to work on writing articles during sessions, and instead I focused my available time at the meeting on information networking. I would set an alarm so that I could be in the hallways between sessions. These informal conversations were my ticket to building relationships that could lead to national service, publication opportunities, and future research collaborations. The sessions themselves were less critical at that meeting. I could request the papers later on anything that I missed. Indeed, the more senior a scholar, the less time spent in the official program of a large conference. Meetings tend to occur in parallel with conference proceedings.

Business books offer suggestions for introverts—people who find the idea of networking to be draining rather than energizing (Lander, 2019; Petrilli, 2012). For example, research indicates that introverts do not recognize faces as much as extroverts, and therefore the impact of informal networking might not be as great.

If striking up a conversation with a stranger invokes anxiety, it is helpful to know the science of networking. At receptions, the best place to meet and talk to people is right after people get a drink from the bar. Researcher and author Vanessa Van Edwards (2017) explored the various places one might stand at a reception—by the entrance, by the food table, in an empty space, and at the end of the drink line. People are most likely and willing to talk after they have a drink in hand. When they arrive, they are still getting their bearings and looking around to see who is there. Food can be awkward and messy, and people may keep leaving. But with a drink in hand, people often do not have a direction to head and are willing to stand and chat a while.

George attended a meeting of one hundred of the most important people in his field. Yet the structure of the meeting did not sufficiently allow for networking. It offered no reception. The meeting was a series of panels with little opportunity for discussion and interaction during the sessions. Lunch was at long rows of tables that were not conducive for meeting people.

With the meeting mainly held in one large hall with everyone present, George considered strategically how he could network in a space not conducive to meeting people. Since there were insufficient stops in the sessions, George noticed that people also were choosing to take breaks themselves by the coffee urn in the back of the room.

George decided to station himself in the back of the room, by the cream and sugar where people tend to pause for a moment. He quietly introduced himself to people he did not know and reconnected with those he did. He had a stack of contact cards to share and followed up later with an email to the connections that he made.

Notice where people are gathering during meetings. Perhaps it is by the book displays. Sometimes it is just outside the doors of a big session. Set a goal to strike up important conversations just outside the "real" meetings.

IDENTIFYING CULTURAL BIASES RELATED TO COMMUNICATION

Perceptions of our communication style impact our ability to build community, make connections, and be heard in collective settings. A growing amount of books advise on how to find the "sweet spot" of assertiveness in business settings, often based on cultural perceptions and intersectional identities. Baseline level of assertiveness is masked by biases that are based on gender, our culture, and our ethnicity as well as our personality. For example, research has found that both men and women criticize women who do not fit within traditional gender or ethnic norms; people approved of assertive dominant black females and White males, but did not approve of White females or black males (Livingston, Rosette, & Washington, 2012, cited in Seltzer, 2015, p. 135). Furthermore, women expect that decisions happen in the meetings; White men tend to expect negotiations to happen in social settings—on the golf course, or when having a drink after the meeting. Inequities can increase when decisions happen in informal settings, since socialization is more likely to occur along gendered and racial lines.

When I was in graduate school studying education policy, I took some courses at the Stanford School of Business. An internationally known professor demonstrated her research on how to map organizational cultures by offering a sketch of the MBA culture at Stanford. The diagram showed the classes, the formal networking opportunities with businesses, and even happy hours. A student raised his hand and questioned, "You don't have golf on there. We don't have classes on Wednesdays. *That's* when we make all of our valuable connections—on the golf course."

Shining a light on these biases is a critical step to problematizing these norms. Critiquing these processes and broadening acceptable behavior improves climate and removes male, White culture as the standard for behavior. Universities should offer training to create awareness of these biases and to reduce discrimination based on cultural biases. Faculty members must be aware of these biases to support and combat them in collaborative dynamics.

Addressing bias can be effective when working with others sharing similar concerns. Collectively affirming one another is a way to have voices heard that might otherwise be silenced. In the Obama administration, for example, female White House officials deliberately affirmed the voices of other women and backed up suggestions made by other female leaders.

Become a student of the unspoken code of communication patterns. It is easy to assume the reasons are personal, but they are often based on structural bias built into interactions and cultures. Clarifying these assumptions and biases helps others to see them. It can also increase one's ability to make choices about when to seek to adapt to a culture and when to challenge it. It provides agency for making tough choices on whether to alter communication styles to make an impact in privileged and biased systems. The following information can be useful when choosing to work within patterns of biases.

Gendered perceptions of "too assertive." Men can act aggressively in business settings, but women have a much narrower scope of what is accepted. Women of color experience an even narrower scope. Women are expected to act "warm" if they are to be heard in collective business settings (Cuddy, Fiske, & Glick, 2008, cited in Mohr, 2015). Warmth and friendliness can be conveyed through efforts to build connection—making small talk at the beginning and end of a meeting, asking people about their personal lives, making jokes, and using nonverbal body language such as smiling, nodding, and mirroring the behaviors of others.

Research also finds that males can make declarative statements, but that women are expected to turn such statements into a question or soften its tone (Mohr, 2015; Seltzer, 2015). For example, a woman would be expected to shift the declarative statement "I recommend we make this choice" to a question: "What would it look like if we made this choice?" or to hedge: "It might be possible to make this choice." The use of "I statements" also softens a tone, such as, "I think that we should make this choice."

Cultural perceptions of "not assertive." Resources for Asian businesspeople working in U.S. contexts advise on how to engage in structures and cultures that have more aggressive and direct forms of interaction (Hyun, 2005). Strategies include practicing making eye contact with others. The resources also coach to prepare for controversy. Be aware of the distinction between what is perceived in the culture as hashing out an idea through disagreement as compared to a personal attack. Gaining a voice in deliberations might be easier by being the first to speak rather than discerning when to jump into an animated discussion. Wait time is shorter in aggressive, extroverted cultures. Getting into the conversation can be challenging. Having comments ready ahead of time can help (Li, Tian, Fang, Xu, Li, & Liu, 2010). Interruption when speaking is another concern in biased settings or places with uneven power dynamics. Research recommends talking as if not interrupted, not making eye contact with the interrupter, and talking at the same rate of speech and volume (Seltzer, 2015).

SUPPORT SPACES: HOW TO FIND MENTORS

A previous section spoke about finding community among groups. This section focuses on one-on-one relationships. Research is extensive on a particular type of professional relationship for faculty—the value of mentors. Mentors help reduce isolation and increase connectedness (Antonio, 2003; Daley, Wingard, & Reznik, 2006; Sims-Boykin, Zambrana, Williams, Salas-Lopez, Sheppard, & Headley, 2003; Stanley, 2006). Through a process of mutual respect and advice, a mentor relationship provides strong ways to build community in a profession. Effective mentors speak clearly and openly about power dynamics (Turner & Myers, 2000; Zuberi & Bonilla-Silva, 2008). They can talk explicitly about bias and advise on paving the way with critical research agendas that focus on marginalized and vulnerable populations (Zambrana et al., 2015). Mentors, therefore, have been shown to be especially beneficial for underrepresented faculty (Griffin et al., 2011; Turner, González, & Wood, 2008; Zambrana et al., 2015). In contrast, a lack of access to effective mentoring is a strong indicator of a lack of retention of underrepresented faculty (Boyd, Cintrón, & Alexander-Snow, 2010; Robinson & Clardy, 2010).

Sometimes departments assign mentors; research suggests this strategy as a way to support junior faculty and especially faculty of color. To be effective in this role, department and colleges should train mentoring faculty on issues of equity and bias and how to support the needs of underrepresented faculty (Zambrana et al., 2015). Underrepresented faculty can find assigned mentorship to be a stressor instead of a support when they feel uncomfortable with faculty dynamics but cannot politically ask to be reassigned. They might even feel pushed into collaborations and activities that do not align with their own career goals and values.

Even when assigned a mentor, you should form your own team of support. No single person can fill all the roles that a person needs. Seek out people who seem like a great fit for your personal needs. Mentors can provide information and introductions to colleagues. They can provide information on the unspoken rules of the academy. They might speak openly

Figure 6.1. Types of Mentors

Confidants: Offer confidential space for asking messy questions
Political Insiders: Explain the politics and unspoken rules of an institution
Connectors: Bring people together
Sponsors: Invite and provide access to formal and informal opportunities
Coaches: Provides focused attention from a trained professional

---

regarding political guidance and social capital. Some provide opportunities; others provide a space for confidential conversations. Mentors can take on various personalities, which I categorize as confidants, political insiders, connecters, sponsors, and coaches (see Figure 6.1).

Confidants allow space for asking questions. They are comfortable with emotion and a lack of clarity. They do not judge but instead provide a source of support. A senior professor who also held administrative responsibilities was my "safe place to land" when I was an assistant professor. An older woman with a background as a guidance counselor, she would shut the door and allow me to be "messy" while processing difficult conversations. She was my advocate, and I trusted my ability to share my worries and mistakes with her.

Political insiders. They understand the dynamics between colleagues and help to explain the unwritten codes of an institution. Savvy, experienced colleagues, these individuals know how processes and politics truly work. I met regularly with an older female, East Asian faculty member to understand the politics of my program, including who did not get along with whom. I shared my tenure dossier with her as well, since she had previously served on the college promotion and tenure committee, and she gave me pointed advice about how to improve my work. She even advised me, "If you are going to have another kid, have it as quickly as possible. You don't want a new baby in your fourth or fifth year." All of her advice was heartfelt, sincere, and golden. I trusted her implicitly.

Connectors. Some mentors make introductions to others and build relationships. My former adviser from graduate school had many research assistants and little time to work with them individually. She built a community structure that included an expectation that students would train and support one another—not just current students but former students as well. She hosted a dinner each year at our discipline's annual meeting. The dinner served as a space to build and to renew ties with the diaspora of academics who shared the experience of working at the same research center at some point in time. This group of professors continues to remain my strongest network of colleagues as I have moved through my professional career—long past the time that our former adviser retired.

Sponsors. They will make suggestions for important roles and vouch for others (Hyun, 2005, p. 216). In my first year on the tenure track, a senior professor invited me to write a chapter for the very prestigious yearbook that he was editing—long before I had established a reputation in my field. He also added me to the associate editors of his journal. He told me what business meetings and associations I should attend and then introduced me, with a strong endorsement, to the people he felt I needed to know at these meetings. I ended up on the executive committee of this association and drew upon my connections in this association for many of my outside letters.

Coaches. Often mentor support is not enough to meet all the needs of an academic. A career-coaching model can lead to greater persistence and retention of individuals pursuing academic careers (Williams et al., 2016a, 2016b). Coaches can allow academics to get sufficient attention and space to make sense of their work climate, to improve their writing process, and to improve success in job searches.

Check the credentials of a potential coach. Hiring a coach trained and certified by an internationally known coaching body can ensure a high quality of training and experience. One way to check for credentials is to see if they are approved by the International Coaching Federation (https://coachingfederation.org).

Coaches and academic consultants can come from a variety of paths to provide their services. Academic coaches and consultants provide a sounding board, feedback, advice on publishing, research, office politics, time management, goal-setting, and work/life balance, among other issues. A traditional coaching model will focus on drawing on wisdom from within the client. Some also have specific emphases, such as improving writing, negotiating jobs, or transitioning to new roles.

OUTSIDE LETTER WRITERS

Tenure-track academics should cultivate a special list of connections—the list of potential outside letter writers and recommenders. The collection of outside letters about a candidate's scholarship is an anxiety-provoking part of tenure and promotion processes. The candidate is asked to select four to five of the most significant pieces of their work to be sent out to notable scholars within their field. Usually candidates can provide a list of potential outside letters, although the institution is always within its purview to go beyond that list to ask other scholars as well.

Figure 6.2. Finding Potential Outside Letter Writers

- Editors of journals who published your work
- Discussants from conferences who expressed enthusiasm for your work
- Editors of yearbooks and other edited volumes who published your work
- People at conferences who come up to you and ask questions
- People who served on review panels that gave you a grant
- People who cite your work

Pre-tenured academics should keep a running list of these potential outside reviewers—from day one after getting a Ph.D. Figure 6.2 offers suggestions for finding potential outside letter writers. The common thread is looking for people who express appreciation and enthusiasm for the candidate.

Academics experience anxiety about the outside reviewer process. It is therefore important to choose them carefully. Reviewers cannot be employed at a candidate's current or previous institutions. They cannot have worked closely with the candidate. They cannot have attended school with the candidate. I have had colleagues tell me that they have even chosen not to write with some scholars in their field pre-tenured because they wanted to ensure that they could list these people as outside reviewers. This strategy might be extreme and should be weighed against the possibility of a collaboration that could lead to a high-quality publication that could count toward tenure.

FINDING BELONGING WITHIN AND BEYOND ACADEMIA

Take stock of the network of places to find belonging and connection. Figure 6.3 provides a worksheet for identifying the people who can form a personal web of belonging. Everyone needs safe places to ask questions, to vent, and to find emotional support. Some of these spaces might be among academics, but it is necessary for most people to construct a life beyond work environments. Finding meaning and value through friendships, family, and passions unrelated to academic work creates a stronger sense of balance and a broader base of support—especially when academic work feels stressful or unstable.

Form a trust circle. Identify the people who can be trusted explicitly and offer a "safe space to land." The list should be small enough to be counted on one hand. The size of the list matters for two reasons—one is that having more than one person is important because different people can provide different kinds of support. But the small number also indicates the need to discern who to trust and to choose these people carefully.

Figure 6.3. Worksheet for Identifying a Web of Support

Collaborators	Mentors
Research Collaborators:	Confidants:
1	1
2	2
Writing Feedback:	Political Insiders:
1	1
2	2
Content Peers:	Connectors:
1	1
2	2
Institutional Peers:	Sponsors:
1	1
2	2

Support beyond academia:
1
2
3
4
5

RECOMMENDATIONS FOR UNIVERSITIES

- Offer targeted leadership training based on departmental cultures and on individual skill sets.
- Provide a formal one-on-one mentoring program for all faculty.
- Develop support structures for underrepresented faculty that include built-in opportunities for critique and input into the design.
- Design support structures that build from the latest research on coaching as a form of professional development.
- Create cohort-model mentoring practices for faculty.
- Hire coaches to work one on one and with cohorts of faculty.

CHAPTER 7

Service

Service work includes responsibilities within the university, the profession, and the community (Lynton, 1995; O'Meara, 2018). *Institutional service* occurs within universities and includes participation on standing committees and building new programs at program, department, college, and university levels. *Professional service* consists of fulfilling a university's outreach mission beyond the university, such as agricultural extension, policy analysis, and continuing education. Faculty also engage in *community service* through civic contributions such as making speeches, serving on boards, and volunteering. *Disciplinary service* includes editorships in journals and leadership in associations. As a career proceeds, expectations increase that these roles in each of these categories will expand to university, national, and international leadership roles.

It is an old adage in the code of academia to "do research, talk service." The common advice continues that no one has been denied a promotion due to *how* they performed their service responsibilities—in part because it is hard to evaluate the quality of the work (Diaz, Garrett, Kinley, Moore, & Schwartz, 2009). Excessive service commitments are perceived as tempering potential publication output, according to most research on succeeding in academia (Blackburn & Lawrence, 1995; Griffin & Reddick, 2011; Tierney & Bensimon, 1996).

Choosing service must therefore be strategic. At all stages of your career, understanding the potential trade-offs of service work is a critical skill in allowing you to choose how to design your work. I suggest that there are three kinds of service responsibilities: (1) service you want to do, because it aligns with your purpose; (2) service you must do, politically; (3) service that you can choose not to do, if you understand how to say no. The text box offers a space to make notes while reading through this chapter.

CHOSEN SERVICE—"WANT-TO-DO" WORK

Connecting service with purpose can help create work responsibilities that can inspire and renew our energies rather than drain them. Service opportunities can build a sense of community among like-minded individuals.

SERVICE DECISION-MAKING CHECKLIST

SERVICE I WANT TO DO:

SERVICE I MUST DO:

SERVICE I WILL SAY NO TO:

Service can also be an avenue to finding sources of belonging. Working on committees can lead to finding support networks and new collaborations (Baez, 2000; Stanley, 2006).

Mentoring graduate students and advanced undergraduates is an important part of the responsibilities of an academic at research-focused institutions. Though often very fulfilling personally, working with students can be time-consuming and emotionally draining, and this work is actually correlated with negative performance reviews (Carrigan, Quinn, & Riskin, 2011; Griffin, Bennett, & Harris, 2013; Link, Swan, & Bozeman, 2008; Misra et al., 2011; O'Meara, Kuvaeva, et al., 2017; Winslow, 2010). It is critical to find ways to mentor students that can model boundaries. Mentoring provides opportunities to share knowledge of the unspoken rules of the academy while supporting students to build their own healthy habits regarding the ABCs of development.

Mentoring and advising is also a responsibility not evenly shared across the academy. Underrepresented faculty often bear greater mentoring and advising loads than other faculty (Griffin & Reddick, 2011; Misra et al., 2011; Mitchell & Hesli, 2013; Porter, 2007; Twale & Shannon,1996). Research suggests that heavier service loads for women lead to a longer time for advancement (Misra et al., 2011; Terosky, O'Meara, & Campbell, 2014), and these trends are even stronger for Black women (Griffin & Reddick, 2011; Stanley, 2006; Turner, 2002). Research indicates that men tend to minimize service work; women tend to seek it out when it aligns with their purpose related to social justice and challenging privilege (O'Meara et al., 2017).

Create clear expectations with student collaborators/research assistants. Try to be as explicit as possible in setting expectations with students. When assigning work, clarify how quickly it is expected to be completed. When they have a question, how should they ask? How many hours will they be working in a week? How much time should they be taking to complete assignments? Model transparency. Ask students to initiate meetings, but set limits on how many. Expect students to bring an agenda to the meeting or to send one ahead of time.

Publish only with students who have the capacity to collaborate. It is not neces-sarily helpful to create the expectation to publish with all students. Instead, consider which students are more likely to pursue academic careers. It is also absolutely fair to consider who might contribute the most, especially as an early-career academic.

Build a "community of practice" of students. Investing in team-building on the front end ensures a quality relationship long-term. Create an expectation that advisees will read one another's work. Agree to only read drafts that have already been read by a peer. Ask senior students to mentor junior stu-dents. Explicitly encourage them to explain the rules of academia, including the rules of writing and publishing. Encourage students to write together.

Triage struggling students. Rather than trying to solve all the problems of struggling students, help them find resources that are broader and deeper than what you can offer yourself. Learning who and where these skill sets are in a university is an act of kindness as well as a way to save enormous blocks of time. Realize also that a struggling student might mean that the fit is wrong—but that student may thrive with another faculty member. Finding that better fit is not necessarily abandoning a student but might be just what they need.

Invite students to stay in touch and reach out to former mentors. My biggest regret in my career has been not keeping in touch with former mentors. "He was too famous to want to hear from me," I thought. "I don't want to bother him." I know now that keeping in touch with former students is a joy of being a professor. Staying connected allows academics to see the growth and outcomes of the people in whom they invested.

Be aware of generational divides. Consider how the age, as well as cultural and gender diversity, of students affects communication and mentorship styles. Even Generation X, Y, and millennial students have different support needs (Bova & Kroth, 2001). Explore whether international students are comfortable asking questions and getting the help that they need. Always remain curious and try not to assume, but also offer space for dissonance and an ability to answer questions.

REQUIRED SERVICE—"MUST-DO" WORK

Some service is a "must-do." Perhaps it is a direct request of a superior, a rotational responsibility that is your turn, or a strategic choice that would help with a future promotion. Understanding the priorities of the institution can help you make these strategic choices.

Must-do service should include the expectation that all faculty engage in equity-focused service. The work of people with privilege can focus on identifying bias among the privileged, whether that be White, male, cisgendered, straight, or able-bodied. The work can also include embracing discomfort and speaking up when injustice occurs—even when that might cause conflict. It should also include increased service by faculty with privilege to balance the extra mentoring load that many underrepresented faculty face.

Mandatory service can still be strategic. That is, keeping your purpose and values at the forefront can give you greater agency in assuming service positions that fit with your sense of agency and career plans. When engaging in service must be done, find the agency to accept positions that would most align with your personal strengths and goals.

Research the stated priorities of the institution. Read the strategic plans of the department/college and the university and think of how your own assets can align with these goals. Choose service options that offer the opportunity to learn valuable skills and access to political influential officials.

Align university service with opportunities to build relationships with senior university official and like-minded people. Service activities can provide opportunities to make connections across campus and to build relationships with potential collaborators. Consider how service might create opportunities to meet like-minded people across the university (Griffin et al., 2011)—especially when working on service that aligns with your purpose.

Melanie was a pre-tenured faculty member, working in a department where most of the undergraduate teaching consisted of teaching required courses for students in other majors. This process left her program with little agency when enrollments started to decline due to shifts in policy made in other places. It also meant that the teaching experience could be frustrating, since many students were not interested in the content of the courses.

Melanie partnered with a colleague to design a new undergraduate major within her department that aligned with the expertise of the faculty. She aligned the mission of the major to fit with identified needs in her college's strategic plan. It was designed to recruit a very different type of student into their college. She benchmarked the major to align with successful programs at other competing universities. This alignment drew positive attention from her dean and her department head.

Work on this project also required collaborating with program faculty and with curricular officials throughout the university. She worked to explain the prospective impact of the program with senior officials to marry the wishes of her department with the bigger political goals of the university. She learned where formal and informal power resided in her institution and also how decision-making processes could be accelerated or stalled.

Melanie was also able to deflect and refuse other potential service roles because of the alignment of this new degree program with the strategic plan of the college and the visibility of the work. Although working on this project took time, the content of the new major aligned with her purpose and therefore felt energizing rather than draining.

Proactively designing and volunteering for service that fits with your own values and skill sets also gives you the ability to say no to other time-heavy requests.

Know what service is more easily recognized and quantifiable. Because it is hard to measure the quality of service work, any ability to show impact or to quantify the results of service work can help communicate the value of the work for promotion and review purposes. It has been suggested, therefore, to prioritize service that is task-oriented, selected competitively, and leadership-focused (Hanasono, Broido, Yacobucci, Root, Peña, & O'Neil, 2019). When possible, ask for a formal title for the assignment—become the recruiting coordinator rather than quietly managing the department alumni list, for example.

SERVICE THAT CAN BE AVOIDED—THE ART OF SAYING NO

Learning to be an academic includes knowing when and how to say no to service duties. For example, though it might be necessary to agree to serve on student doctoral committees within a department, that does not mean that you have to agree to serve on all student committee requests made from outside of the department.

Learn the art of negotiation to find service that fits personal needs according to your purpose and political goals. Negotiation takes practice and can include both practicing the creation of boundaries and negotiation in lower-stakes situations to learn how to exercise these muscles. It involves establishing boundaries, renegotiating previous service commitments, and creatively suggesting alternative solutions. Practicing with a coach or a colleague before engaging in a high-stakes conversation with a superior about a negotiation is highly recommended.

Doug was a mid-career faculty member who had just been promoted to professor. He had successfully completed rotations as his department chair, as well as serving as a college-wide curriculum coordinator. He was known for running an efficient meeting and for effectively reducing tensions between colleagues.

When the department head announced she was stepping down, the dean turned to Doug as a natural successor. Colleagues also pressed him to apply, since another colleague was gunning for the position but was not well regarded by fellow faculty.

Doug sought coaching to discern whether an administrative position was a fit with his sense of purpose and his personal career trajectory. He was a prolific scholar and had several projects that he wanted to complete in the next few years. He also had two children still in school. He valued the flexibility of completing his work around transportation needs and having time in the summer and in the afternoons to be the primary caregiver.

Doug struggled with the awareness that he was the best choice for the position in his department. He came to realize, however, that just because he was the most qualified for a position, he did not have to take it. In other words, just because he fit the position well did not mean that the position fit him.

I worked with Doug to develop a set of negotiation strategies to prepare him for a conversation with his dean. He explained his responsibilities in other pieces of his life and suggested that it was not quite the right time in his career for this position but did not rule out the possibility in the future.

Doug also offered a creative third-way solution to the dilemma. Since none of the current faculty seemed to fit the leadership role at that time, he offered to chair an external search to find a strong leader for the department. He could use his leadership skills to find a replacement rather than being the replacement himself.

Say no, relentlessly. Limit optional requests, such as guest lecturing. Strategically choose opportunities that have the greatest visibility and that align with your purpose. Learn what meetings are required and which ones can be skipped. Women are less likely to say no than men (O'Meara, Kuvaeva, et al., 2017). Practice saying no in many ways. A way to say no can be couched in an affirmation of the request—"I'd love to, but . . ." or . . . "Thank you for thinking of me." Your response can also be said more firmly to prevent future requests. Figure 7.1 includes a range of examples of how to say no.

Acknowledging when your batteries are depleted. Even when service does align with your purpose, know when enough is enough. To do the work that matters, it is critical to preserve a margin of energy. When your batteries are depleted, emotional and physical hardships multiply. Depletion leads to physical illness, damage to relationships, and the burdens of shame and stress.

Practice learning to say no within personal relationships if the workplace feels too intimidating, or begin in the workplace if family relationships are too much of a challenge as a start. I have been working on this process with my own family. When I know I have depleted myself, I tell them, "I have nothing left! I need to recharge my batteries before we have

Figure 7.1. Examples of Saying No

- I would love to come to your class in the future, but my calendar is too full this semester.
- Thank you, but I cannot take on that project at this time.
- What an important issue. I'm very supportive but cannot commit now.
- Thank you for thinking of me. I'll get back to you when I have time to commit to this issue.
- I am in the middle of writing an important paper that I need to complete before my annual review. I need to focus all of my energy in that direction for the next few months.
- Once I have tenure, I would love to.
- With my busy schedule, I can no longer participate.
- Given my responsibilities, I am unable to say yes for the foreseeable future.
- My schedule is too full to take that on.

(List adapted from James, 2014; Rockquemore & Laszloffy, 2008; Seltzer, 2015)

this conversation." Such conversations do not always go well. The response from needy children is much like needy faculty at times: "How dare you take a break from being a mother?" Demonstrating these boundaries is healthy, though. For me and for my children. And for my colleagues as well.

MID-CAREER ACADEMICS: CREATIVELY BROADENING CONTRIBUTION

Mid-career professors often face an emotional low in their career satisfaction. Research indicates that faculty satisfaction and retention are strongly related to encouraging creativity in faculty and valuing a broader range of research contribution in the form of public engagement and service to society (Neumann, 2009). Mid-career faculty tend to find that they need some new pathway to find renewed inspiration by developing a new avenue to share their expertise.

Many faculty begin working in university administration at this stage of their careers. Doing so can provide them with a space to share the wisdom they have developed over their careers and to grow a new set of skills. For other faculty, administration does not feel like a great fit. This section focuses on other pathways to mid-career fulfillment that faculty might choose. This extra work can take on a range of formats, including consulting, speaking, serving as expert witnesses, and writing books for profit.

Marilyn had been promoted to professor 6 years before. When administrative positions opened up at her university, she was always asked if she would be willing to apply. But her gut always made her feel that she should step away from these opportunities. Yet she was feeling mid-career ennui and finding that her previous motivations for her work no longer fit. I encouraged her to revisit the exercises from Chapter 4, "Agency," with a fresh eye on what was coming up in the present moment, rather than how she has always described her work in the past.

I worked with Marilyn, through a series of reflections, on the type of values that were important in her current working environment. A prolific writer, she preferred the ownership of designing quality research over supervising colleagues. Yet she longed for something more that she could grow. Although the lure of extra salary was tempting with an administrative position, through a series of brainstorming exercises, she decided to try to market herself as a consultant to companies that could benefit from her technological expertise. She clarified the conflict-of-interest policies with her university, advertised her consulting work, and found a way to procure a small, steady side income in addition to her work as a professor.

Depending on the university, academics can make use of their unique skill set to obtain additional income through paid consulting, sometimes called a "side hustle." This process can provide them with alternative ways to fulfill their purpose and expand their creativity without as much restriction from external forces and bureaucratic politics.

The public scholarship aspect of being a faculty member means that a component of this work might even be encouraged by universities—or it might be prohibited. University-related policies regarding earning extra income, including conflict-of-interest guidelines, must be followed. Frank conversations about the nature of the work ahead of time with university officials is critical to avoid any unintended actions that could be grounds for violations. For universities that prohibit profit ventures of faculty, it can be possible to find ways to shift workload within a job to find greater fulfillment. Some scholars negotiate entrepreneurial work as service credit in place of other service that is less inspiring. For universities that permit paid consulting, be sure where and how title and university affiliation can be used to promote other work. Keeping the work separate is also critical—which means not conducting the freelance work when at the university.

Pay close attention to how hours worked relate to dollars earned. Many professors rarely think in terms of business models of time and product, and it might be a skill that has to be actively developed. The task can be challenging, since the goal is marketing oneself—learning how to describe complicated concepts in a clear manner to industry, for example. If finding a side hustle is of interest, draw on the endless supply of business texts focusing on marketing and entrepreneurship to learn how to hone a product and to find clients.

RECOMMENDATIONS FOR UNIVERSITIES

- Increase the expectation and value of equity-focused service.
- Design opt-out systems for time-intensive administrative roles. A rotation of critical roles among faculty develops a shared sense of expectation and equitable load. For example, in my department, the program chairs rotate through all members of the tenured faculty.
- Develop clear benchmarks for performance and accountability for service expectations in areas such as advising and committee work. In one effort to improve clarity, a coalition of universities even revised policies to assign different levels of service credit for low, medium, and high time-intensive service roles (O'Meara, 2018). For example, chairing a committee received greater credit than serving on a committee.
- Create processes by which a broader range of service can be documented, and provide guidance on how to articulate and document service impact as a part of ongoing information on tenure and promotion policies (Diaz et al., 2009).
- Increase transparency to make work processes more equitable. Share information across departments regarding faculty workload, including ranges for course load, committee responsibilities, and administrative roles. Support dialogue about department-wide workload to encourage a greater equitable distribution (O'Meara, 2018).

CHAPTER 8

Competencies

While the "absent-minded professor" may be a trope, the thread of truth beneath the caricature is real for many. The freedom of academia can allow for endless unstructured time, but with aggressive expectations of a publication deadline. Without skills in time management, achieving career goals can be a challenge.

Academics must impose a rigorous discipline of routine to writing regularly and often and to learning to minimize the time required of other academic responsibilities. They must maintain a narrow focus, be relentless, and have a plan. It is easy to feel a false perception of plenty of time to get research completed. With 5 to 6 years on the tenure track (depending on the institution and how time is counted), time might feel abundant. Adjunct, fixed-term, and faculty not at research institutions may have even less time to complete their research and writing due to a heavier teaching load.

Competencies consist of the skills and abilities needed to achieve success (Mitra, 2004; Villarruel & Lerner, 1994). Learning is a process of working toward learning new skills and habits. The secret to building competencies is the belief in oneself that these skills can be honed.

A *growth mindset* (Dweck, 2007, 2010) perceives achievements and goals instead to be something that can be learned through dedication and hard work. With a focus on agency, a growth mindset offers a signpost to design a future path. It encourages a process of learning how organizations work and having the ability to make choices. Tasks can be explored in new ways, discipline can be deepened, and it is possible to learn new skills and ways of being. Intelligence and innate talent are only a starting point that must be built on with effort. This perspective encourages resilience, motivation, and improved productivity. It creates pathways to success.

In contrast, a *fixed mindset* draws on the inner critic, leading to beliefs such as "I'm not good enough. I don't belong here." For example, coming from a fixed mindset, it is more likely to internalize the comments of peer reviewers as a sign of our ability and worthiness rather than as a process for learning how to improve. Mistakes then become something to hide because it is assumed that improvement is not possible. Fixed mindset perspectives do not recover well from setbacks. Rather than learning and moving forward, setbacks inspire a fixed mindset to retreat and to decrease effort.

GOAL-SETTING

Goal-setting is essential for finding agency within academic settings and connects purpose to action. It also reduces time stressors that increase baseline stress and anxiety levels. Goal-setting is vital for finding agency within academics because it keeps faculty tethered to purpose and values, and time stressors increase baseline stress and anxiety levels that impact all aspects of career success.

Developing a goal-setting process for a career requires understanding the broader picture of work/life balance. A solid work/life balance should provide stable or increased agency, accuracy, innovation, and patience (Morgenstern, 2004b). The wheel of life (see text box) offers a visual representation of work/life balance. The wheel helps us to think of balance as involving more than two spheres of work and home, and instead finding coherence across the multiple identities held by each individual.

WORK/LIFE BALANCE ASSESSMENT

The Wheel of Life offers a visual examination of all aspects of your life. A sample wheel is offered below. Use the sample to create your own wheel, with as many pie wedges as you need. Assign pieces of the wheel to important parts of your life. You choose the categories. Include work categories such as research productivity and teaching/service work. Include meaningful relationships with family members and friends. Include play, health, and faith. Fill in your level of satisfaction with each of these categories. It is not realistic to expect fulfillment in all categories at any point in time. Some will be brimming over; others will feel empty. Celebrate what is working in your life. Set goals where you want to make changes. Watch the inner-critic "shoulds" creeping in here. The details within that balance should be specialized for each person and not based on expectations of others.

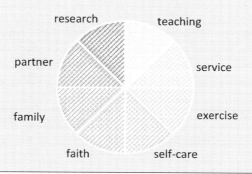

Aaliyah used the work/life balance tool to assess the parts of her life that were feeling fulfilled and in need of greater work. She found her health, spiritual practices, and recreational time to be lacking, so she set the following goals:

- Start a running routine 2–4-miles twice per week with a friend
- Practice mindfulness everyday [twice a day for 30 minutes]
- Weekdays: maintain good routine of going to bed by 11:30 p.m., and getting up by 6:30 a.m.
- Talk to one long-distance family/friend every week
- Schedule a coffee date with a mentor/sponsor once per month

While on the job market, doctoral students actively seek evidence of faculty having balanced lives. Research indicates that universities lose top candidates when it appears that faculty are not able to juggle academia with other demands and identities (Mason, Goudlen, & Frasch, 2009; Philipsen & Bostic, 2010; Rice et al., 2000). Having a critical departmental mass of academics who have children was pointed as one metric to measure how supportive a department might be of balancing multiple identities as a scholar (Philipsen & Bostic, 2010).

Mikayla had two job offers. One institution had an office dedicated to placing spouses in both academic and nonacademic positions. A second only mailed her a page in the phone book as its only support for helping her partner find a job in an isolated college town. The first institution had a dedicated office of support for trailing partners—including those not on the tenure track. The support of her partner's job search played a very important role in Mikayla's decision. The spousal-hire office worked with him for 6 months, identifying positions within the large university that might fit, speaking with the hiring committees to learn about the fit, and advising him on how to apply for the positions. Mikayla reported that she and her partner felt great loyalty and appreciation to the university for their efforts and that this in turn has caused them to feel very engaged in their new positions.

Happiness of perceived work/life balance varies based on gender and ethnicity (Denson, Szelényi, & Bresonis, 2018). Black women report less work/life balance than Black men, but Latina women report more balance than Latino men. Single White faculty with no children were much less likely to have work/life balance than married White faculty with children. Department and institutional support for work/life balance issues was found to be the strongest positive predictor of perceived work/life balance for all faculty. Increased spending on research led to improved perception of work/life balance across race, ethnicity, and gender.

Mary was highly discouraged from taking maternity leave by her department chair and older male colleagues because it would be inconvenient to them. The faculty was short-staffed and did not know how to cover her classes. Being pre-tenured, she felt obligated to heed the pressure from her chair and not take the leave. Making such choices, however, impacted not only her quality of life and research output, but also women after her who then wanted to take leave but did not have the example and history of previous women making use of the policy. Mary therefore suffered the pressure of doing what she felt was necessary politically in her immediate situation, while going against what she believed was just and that could also support other women. Now post-tenure, she actively speaks up against such behavior and mentors junior female—and male—faculty to take the leave that they are due.

Structural components of working an academic job can interfere with work/life balance. Single faculty struggle to find partners once accepting a tenure track position (Philipsen & Bostic, 2010). Dual academic couples struggle with finding a home for both partners that allows job satisfaction.

One of the major ways that the COVID-19 pandemic has exacerbated inequity was the stress that it placed on work/life balance. Data are just beginning to show the ways in which the burdens of working with children at home and the closing down of research labs and data collection will have long-term impacts on academics. Evidence is just emerging of the extent to which women in particular bear these burdens.

Even prior to the pandemic, marriage and having children both negatively impacted a women's ability to acquire tenure-track positions and to gain tenure, compared to male counterparts (Wilson, 2012). Women on the tenure track also were less likely to have children as compared to men on the tenure track (Mason & Goulden, 2004). Although men and women are beginning to share responsibilities in academic families when looking at early-career men and women (Philipsen & Bostic, 2010, p. 32), the impact of parenting on female faculty still remains a burden, with women taking on the majority of parenting duties, with negative impacts on balancing workload and career progress, including a negative impact on research time (Misra, Lundquist, & Templer, 2012) and a reduced ability of women to publish when parenting preschool-aged children (Stack, 2004). Men are doing more to share in the balance of domestic duties in academic families, but men still tend to overinflate their contribution compared to their partners', according to empirical research. Despite these challenges, research indicates that life satisfaction is greater for women who seek out balanced success in their professional and family lives. Women who identified as focusing on success in both spheres reported feeling more satisfied about their lives and experiencing less stress.

Although this research seems dated in a world of increased remote work, successful balance has been shown to include keeping strict boundaries between professional and personal lives. Research also recommends being fully present for family or work and not trying to blend them (Galinsky, Sakai, & Wigton, 2011; Seltzer, 2015). Yet the COVID-9 pandemic necessitated working from home in ways that the blending of work and family became unavoidable. Rather than keeping boundaries between spheres, academics needed to rethink how to find restoration while juggling workloads and family. With the expectation that faculty teaching may never be the same, academics face a time of transition of work and family identities.

TIME MANAGEMENT: "PLAN YOUR WORK, WORK YOUR PLAN"

Be a student of one's own daily rhythms. Protect morning hours if that is the most productive time. Consider which weekdays have the most space to complete research and which days are better suited to meetings and teaching. Reflect on what times of the year have the most uninterrupted time for writing (for me, these are term breaks and weeks 2 through 6 of each semester). Other months may be too busy, and it will be hard to get much writing done at all, such as the last month of each academic semester.

Examinations of the daily schedules of famous writers show the regularity of their quality worktime (Oshin, 2017). Stephen King and Alice Munro have a quota of pages per day—they both write five pages a day. Maya Angelou wrote from 7 a.m. to 2 p.m. every weekday. The schedules demonstrate these authors' choices of work/life balance, because they all include a set time to spend with loved ones and for exercise. Charles Darwin, for example, took three walks a day.

Create a visual publishing pipeline. Begin planning time by getting clarity on the most important tasks. Map them out visually and create a plan for completion. Include the time needed to complete each piece of the process. Create a computer file or use a visual whiteboard. Revisit this pipeline every month. Share it on social media to make yourself accountable.

Figure 8.1 offers an example of a pre-tenured professor pipeline. Hana keeps a publishing plan that leads up to the date she turns in her materials for review. Her visual pipeline includes not just what she is writing, but her journal and conference targets as well. Hana publishes her pipeline on her social media regularly as an accountability mechanism.

From her visual pipeline, Hana was able to map backward to develop a "to-do" list as she prepared for the work she was going to do during the break between academic semesters (Figure 8.2). Called backward design (Childre, Sands, & Pope, 2009), this mapping process takes longer-term

Figure 8.1. Hana's Research Pipeline

Manuscripts in progress	Manuscripts out	Conferences	Invited lectures
"Partnerships" article—finish implications	"Teaching" article—in press	AERA—April, Toronto	Student voice meeting, May
"Statewide" article—develop draft before April Conference	"Advisor" article—under review/next target: EJ journal	IJSV—May, Philadelphia	Melbourne study group, October
"Method" study—data collected	"Micropolitics" article—accepted	UCEA—October, Houston	

Figure 8.2. Hana's To-Do List From Her Pipeline for Intersession Break

☐ Write a draft of journal article and set up a planning meeting next week with my collaborator (research)
☐ Analyze data for method study (research)
☐ Generate a list of book reviewers for my journal (service)
☐ Prep syllabi for two new courses (teaching)

goals and breaks them into achievable chunks of work that happen in a measured pace over a long period of time. Appendix B provides additional examples of mapping a workload pipeline onto 2-week task lists.

Assign time needed for each of the tasks on the list. Develop an awareness of how long tasks take and map these tasks onto the calendar. Make this a quick process for each week—but beware of spending more time planning than actually writing. People who lack organization would benefit from greater structure. However, those who gain comfort from structure and lists can sometimes use them as a way to procrastinate and work on the list rather than the writing.

Create a schedule. Building a time map to reshape time use (see Figure 8.3 for a time map of a mid-career professor with two children, adapted from Morgenstern, 2004a). Rather than using a specific calendar for a week, Morgenstern suggests beginning with a broader sketch of the structure of your days. Assign categories to blocks of time—teaching, writing, self-care, and errands. It helps to sort similar tasks into groups; it gives you a sense of the shape of a week and helps you clarify priorities.

Figure 8.3. Sample Time Map (Main Work Times Shaded)

Time	Monday	Tuesday	Wednesday	Thursday	Friday
7:00	email	email	email	email	email
8:00	child/house	child/house	child/house	child/house	child/house
9:00	exercise	exercise	exercise	exercise	exercise
10:00	research	email/service	research	email/service	research
11:00		meetings		meetings	
noon		teach		teach	
1:00					
2:00			errands		
3:00	email/service		walk dog	meetings	email/service
4:00	child pick up	child pick up	child pick up	child pick up	child pick up
5:00	walk dog	walk dog	soccer carpool	walk dog	walk dog
6:00	dinner	dinner		dinner	dinner
7:00					
8:00					
9:00	email	email	email	email	email
10:00	bed	bed	bed	bed	bed

IDENTIFYING SELF-CARE

Self-care moments should be a way of recharging one's batteries. Looking at the categories of physical health, escape, and people (Morgenstern, 2004b), consider what activities would most energize and refuel. Get enough sleep to allow the mind to function fully—usually 7–9 hours, according to research (Nagoski & Nagoski, 2020). Schedule enough physical activity to calm the brain and make time for play and joy.

Self-care also includes permission to be fully present when with family and friends. It means screen-free time. It means permission to turn off—even engaging in a technology "sabbath"—a commitment to one day a week away from all forms of screens to re-plug into relationships.

Self-care requires a critical examination of numbing versus real re-charging. Research indicates that activities that truly recharge can take only 10 minutes—yoga or medication, listing 10 things for which you are grateful, appreciating another person (Seltzer, 2015). Longer activities may actually numb rather than recharge. Numbing does not occur selectively—it removes the positive emotions as much as it does the negative (Brown, 2018) and cuts oneself off from life. Watching one guilty pleasure television episode

Figure 8.4. Numbing Versus Recharging

Separate a page of paper into halves, labeling them Numbing and Recharging.
Using words, images, and cuttings from magazines, list the ways that you numb
on the one side and the ways that you truly recharge on the other. Display in
a place where you might stop yourself from numbing and choose to recharge
instead.

NUMB	RECHARGE
Examples: Binge-watching television, eating a pint of ice cream, smoking, social media scrolling	*Examples: Taking a walk, deep breaths, meditation, laughter, talking to a close friend*

(Adapted from Brown, 2018)

may provide a needed mental break; binge-watching an entire season instead may cause a feeling of numbing and dissatisfaction. The text box offers a process for learning about recharging and numbing activities.

Work/life balance should be visible. Schedule recharging activities in your
time map. Controlling your own destiny also comes with the responsibility
of taking care of yourself. Although academic work offers the privilege of
flexible deadlines, it also means that it lacks external structure. Often what
falls off the table is self-care.

Track work time. Find a simple way to log writing hours during the weekly
review and seek to protect and even increase them. Review each week and
compare actual time spent to planned time. Prioritizing quality work time
also means noticing how much time is spent on other tasks, including teaching preparation, service, social media, and television. Phone apps can monitor how much time is being spent across projects. Designed for consultants,
such an app could be useful for documenting work/life balance, writing
versus teaching preparation time, and other ways to assess whether use of
time aligns with personal values and goals.

Create a weekly review plan. Some organizational experts suggest assessing the week before it begins. Rockquemore and Laszloffy (2015, p. 96) call
this process the "Sunday meeting." The intention of such a weekly review
is to look at the week overall, compare it to the larger plan, and adjust.
Activities during this weekly time can include the following:

- Check in with how planned work aligns with personal purpose and
  values.
- Review your 5-year plan and adjust the master time map.
- Rate productivity and overall satisfaction for the past week.

- Revise previously unrealistic timelines.
- Intentionally check in each week with your inner critic and take the time to mindfully ask it to step aside.
- Revise the publishing pipeline and tasks for this week. Ensure that sufficient time for writing is protected. Consider whether additional writing time is possible this week.
- Note specific appointments that cannot be moved.
- Assess the to-do list beyond the publishing pipeline. Consider which tasks can be delayed or removed (see below).

DELETE, DELAY, DELEGATE, DIMINISH

When evaluating the benefit of a task, see whether the word *should* emerges. Then ask, "Who is speaking in this moment? Is it my inner critic or my inner mentor?" You can learn how to identify the *shoulds* by using Julie Morgenstern's (2011) process of "Deleting, Delaying, Delegating, and Diminishing" (adapted in Figure 8.5).

"Delete" the items on a schedule that are a **should** ***instead of a*** **must.** Skip optional lectures and unnecessary meetings. Stop adding more detail to student comments than is necessary. Stop opening social media reflexively. Notice the increase in energy when making a decision—that is a sign that you have made the right choice.

"Delay" items on a separate part of the to-do list. Keep track of items that can wait for another day. Include items that you have assigned to others and for which you are awaiting a response. Delaying can often mean that issues diminish or even disappear.

It took me a long time to understand the value of delaying responses to some email. I had the luxury of a sabbatical recently, and I turned on a vacation message that indicated that I would not be responding to emails quickly since I was not on duty that semester. I soon realized how well people could solve their own problems with a bit of time. Solutions that I would have spent time working on were often not necessary after a few

Figure 8.5. Strategies for Finding More Time

Delete: What tasks can you just simply eliminate without retribution?
Delay: What items can be put on hold?
Delegate: What work can be given to others?
Diminish: How can you create shortcuts and streamline tasks?

(Adapted from Morgenstern, 2011)

days—people figured out their own answers if I gave them a few days to let problems "season."

"Delegate" tasks that others can do. Give assistants tasks such as copy-editing, tracking down citations, and researching specific content. Consider what household chores can be done by others to maximize your writing time during busy periods. Decide when to spend the money to hire others with the question: What tasks can others do that would significantly decrease my level of stress?

Alison sought coaching because she was burnt out. She struggled with the inner critic images of the perfect mom and the successful academic pre-tenured. Looking at her internal rhythms, she was keenly aware that her most efficient writing hours were between 2 p.m. and 6 p.m. She struggled with the limiting belief that they were the "most important" parenting hours of the day (an idea that seeped into my brain as an inner critic from some parenting book). They were certainly the most challenging parenting hours, and if she was fully honest, they were some of the least satisfying hours of parenting for her. They involved low energy for everyone and lots of frustrating errands—driving to activities, meal preparation, and homework time.

When on a deadline for a publication, grant, and during the critical year before her dossier was due, Alison invested in child care several days a week during these key hours. She asked the babysitter to clean the kitchen and prepare dinner for the children and to transport the kids from place to place.

Her sense of accomplishment increased and her stress declined. She emerged from her writing cave on those days with a sense of professional accomplishment. She was much less likely to procrastinate, knowing that she was paying for that time.

She was also ready to fully engage with her children, rather than burdened by the tasks of parenthood of transition and mealtime preparation. On her best days, Alison gave herself permission to appreciate this gift of child care rather than feeling guilty about it, knowing that these days of pressure would not last forever but were instead a finite period of time in her career and her kids' lives.

"Diminish" emails. Handle emails with efficiency and read files only once. Respond to items requiring less than 10 minutes of your time immediately. Be precise in the subject line to improve the efficiency of the emails that must be sent (Morgenstern, 2011). Move longer-term items to folders and add the tasks to the to-do list. An inbox should not be the to-do list, since the order of items cannot be controlled easily. Keep focused on priorities and use a to-do list faithfully instead of email to decide the next task. Beware also

---

TIME MANAGEMENT CHECKLIST

☐ Assess work/life balance with the wheel exercise.
☐ Create a visual research pipeline.
☐ Develop a time map to commit to finishing the work.
☐ Commit to a weekly check-in to assess productivity goals and to
   adjust.

---

of the virus that is "zeroing out the inbox" rather than completing more important work.

"Diminish" schedule gaps. Diminishing can also occur by stacking meetings. Figure 8.3 (earlier in this chapter) showed an example of a stacked schedule of combining similar tasks throughout the week. Meet with students on your own schedule, not theirs. That might mean that people have to wait a few days to schedule a meeting. Stack meetings around teaching duties to limit spare office time. Have days accountable only to the long-term plans—days of writing, research, and visioning.

The summary checklist in the text box summarizes a set of tasks that can move work to completion—visual pipelines, time maps, weekly check-ins, and work/life balance assessments.

PRODUCTIVITY

"Your calendar will show what you value" is a useful metric for the task of prioritizing work. Important goals should be visible, regular, and protected. They should be visible in the calendar.

Protecting peak research time. Identify the time of day and the week when quality work seems to flow the easiest. Treat this time like gold. Do the toughest and most important work then, whatever that might be. Consciously acknowledge the task that is your biggest stressor and get it done. Such tasks can leave a knot in your stomach when ignored.

Making a dent in that huge task will lead to greater satisfaction than completing 10 other things. "Pay yourself first" is a slogan used to consider how to organize a day and complete hard work first. Do not check the easy items off the "to-do" list. Do the hard stuff. Tackling such projects will ease anxiety and give you greater control over your schedule. Mastering this skill will lead to steady progress on your goals by building discipline toward tackling the difficult tasks.

Remaining focused on the main ideas might involve developing a strategy for listing the easier work that can happen later. Keep a list of work to be done later. Such lists might be helpful when you are writing documents and field notes. For example, when doing the deep work of writing a first draft, I use comment bubbles in a word processing document as a way to make a running list on the side of the page of tasks that can be done later when it is not golden writing time—tasks such as "Look up this citation. Need another example here. Did I get this association correct? Who else wrote about this?" These comment bubbles create a to-do list of tasks that can be completed at other times in my week. With even 5 minutes, I can answer a comment bubble in my own writing. This process allows the ideas to flow and helps you keep the inner critic at bay.

Create conductive work conditions. Note the conditions that make important work easier to accomplish. Music can help you connect with a particular mood or mindset (Wehrenberg, 2016). Consider using the same playlist when working on a project over a few months to see if it helps you stay focused. Or consider using a white noise machine if music is distracting.

Gerry listens to Pink Floyd when he is blocked in his writing; it somehow makes the writing processes flow better because of the habit of listening to the same music over time. He doesn't even listen to Pink Floyd otherwise. He just knows that the music works for him when he needs the writing juices to flow. His family has heard the lyrics to the album "Delicate Sound of Thunder" far too often when he is on a book deadline. They even have family jokes about it.

Also note common blocks and barriers to successful work time. Often people make up rules in their heads that prevent productive times from happening: "I can't write until my inbox is empty" or "I have to clean my kitchen before I can begin writing."

Note what distractions decrease focus. A text message. A pop-up notification on the computer screen. Alarms and buzzes and bells and whistles that can be turned off.

Develop rewards for longer times of productivity. Set a timer to stay focused longer. Save enjoyable habits as rewards when you complete a project. Savor the victory.

Kim loves jigsaw puzzles in the winter, but once she starts a puzzle, she gets obsessed, and hours of time can pass as she focuses on the pieces. When on a deadline, she will not allow herself to open a jigsaw puzzle until she sends the draft out. Once the deliverables are sent, she cracks open a puzzle and celebrates.

Experiments to Improve Productivity

Taking on some challenges to alter usual rhythms can provide experiments in how to improve work quality and to shrink the amount of time necessary to complete work. Some experiments to try are listed below. Check the ones you are going to try.

☐ **Do not open email until after completing substantive work.** Protect your most valuable time. Complete heaviest writing work before opening email. Only check email once or twice a day.

☐ **Shrink "meaningful work" windows.** Finding time also includes changing mental models of how much time is needed for quality work, and especially writing. Research indicates that regular writing, and writing each day, can be more efficient than blocking out long stretches of time once or twice a week (Bolker, 1998; Zerubavel, 1999). Create a challenge of seeing how small of a time window can be used for meaningful work. Even half an hour is enough to write one paragraph. Try breaking your own record for efficiency in small time periods.

☐ **Ride the energy flow.** Dive in deep for short spurts of time when you are feeling especially productive. Find a period of time when energy is particularly high and the work is flowing; honor this energy shift and write as much as possible. Ride the inspiration wave. Ask for support from loved ones. Such a wave of energy will not last forever, so treasure it and slide into the flow of writing.

☐ **Create a "meaningful work" cocoon.** Stick to set hours when available for interruptions by family members, colleagues, and students. People dropping by to chat can eat away at productivity. If you are working at home, create an understanding with roommates and family as to when disruptions are okay and when they are not.

☐ **Create accountability structures.** Build communities of support and rely on them (see Chapter 6, "Belonging"). Write in the company of others. Trade work regularly to give feedback. Hire a coach to help to prioritize goals and stick to them.

☐ **End each "meaningful work" session with a note on how to jump in and get started substantively.** Note right there in the writing document where to begin the next time. For example, "Add two more examples and then write the conclusion." Create a clear task as a starting-off point.

Whether it be mastering your schedule, creating boundaries, or trying new ways of writing, the goal is to become a student of your rhythms and habits. Note the false barriers created in the mind to block productivity. Be brave and try on new habits.

Not all work is meaningful work. Having ambitious goals in your career must include understanding spaces to take it slower. Some activities are easier to accomplish in the early stages of a career, some in the middle, and some at the end. Perhaps it is possible to have it all, but not all at once. By pulling back to a wide-angle view of your lifespan, it is possible to make better choices about how to show up in the moment of any phase of life, and to be fully present within it, rather than lamenting the goals that are best accomplished at other times.

Within a given year, it is also true that not all academic responsibilities can be an A+ effort, just like all parts of life cannot be embraced at 100% energy. Becoming a student of your institution and also maintaining alignment with your own values and purpose can help you triage potential work into priorities. Learn the formula for what work must be exceptional and what just needs to be a passing grade. Some other work can fall off the table entirely. This knowledge can help you make choices based on how activities address personal values or institutional priorities. For example, at some research-focused (R1) institutions, research and writing must be top-notch but other work might have less value. The balance of what must be excellent varies from institution to institution.

I attended a panel of faculty discussing how to successfully review journal articles. I was shocked by the range of time that faculty would commit to the service work of peer-reviewing an article. Some faculty spent one hour; others spent days on a review.

As an editor of a peer-reviewed journal, I expect a review to find three to five issues that can improve this paper. More than three to five actually makes it harder for an author to have a direction in how to improve the work. That task should not take more than a few hours at most. While I appreciate the reviewers who provide line edits and seek clarification on clauses and confusing sentences, those types of reviewers go above and beyond what I expect. My excellent copyeditor can do that work.

As a pre-tenured academic, do what is expected from an editor. Going above and beyond can be saved for post-tenure, if then!

RECOMMENDATIONS FOR UNIVERSITIES

- Offer professional development for improving writing quality for publication and for grants.
- Encourage department chairs/leaders to shield junior faculty from unnecessary meetings.
- Teach junior faculty explicitly what meetings and events they must attend versus what meetings and events are optional.
- Question the purposes of meetings and consider if the tasks are better completed online or in a shorter format.
- Provide job-search assistance for dual-career couples.
- Question why tenure must be based on the same amount of time for every faculty member and explore potential biases in that sameness; examine policies such as part-time tenure-track options.
- Expand reasons why the tenure clock can be paused and why teaching loads can be reduced—ensure that clock-stopping is gender-neutral and that faculty are *encouraged* to use the policy without any fear of retribution or penalty.
- Have faculty "opt out" of stopping a tenure/promotion clock rather than "opting in."
- Offer on-site, quality child care and allow part-time child care options.
- Extend leave to fathers and adoptive parents of both genders.
- Provide leadership development for chairs/department heads on work/life balance issues.

CHAPTER 9

Teaching

Becoming an effective teacher requires a return to the framework of this book—understanding structures and deepening your own sense of purpose. It requires mastering your own inner critics and skill sets. It also requires seeing and pushing against bias embedded in classroom settings. By attending to these processes, you make it possible to model for students what this book attempts to teach to academics. It is then possible to make visible the hidden structures of the academy, including bias and inequities, and to help young people build the skill sets needed for success. This chapter takes these four concepts in turn—learning to stifle inner critics for teachers, identifying competencies needed to be a successful teacher, understanding contexts that create biased classroom structures, and learning how to empower students through equity-focused instruction strategies.

GETTING RID OF INNER CRITICS IN THE CLASSROOM

Beyond the larger issues of systemic bias, struggles with teaching may be due to inexperience. Some scholars begin teaching without having previous experience in graduate school or otherwise. Somehow it is assumed that academics will know how to teach, even though most are not specially trained. Mid-career professors can also find their inner critic flaring in classroom settings when they are teaching new courses, using new formats, or returning to teaching after a break in administration.

Imposter syndrome is a common name for an inner critic that often affects new teachers. It happened to me on my first day of teaching 1st grade long ago. The minute I wrote my name on the board, 6-year-old Tessa raised her hand and told me, "That's not teacher handwriting!" I was outed before I began.

IMPROVED CONFIDENCE IN THE CLASSROOM

Command respect. A lack of organization can be misinterpreted as a lack of ability. Act the part. Dress more formally than other faculty if feeling insecure about teaching. Err on the side of firm deadlines and a lack of late work options, since it is easier to loosen guidelines than to tighten them later. Respect includes being responsible for student learning and is not the same as formality. Think of excellent teachers from movies and personal history. Consider how they maintained boundaries while also showing that they cared about their job of making sure that learning was occurring.

Create expectations of formality. With research indicating a tendency for students to take women and faculty of color less seriously in the classroom (Lewis & Richmond, 2010), early-career women and faculty of color especially dislike when students engage in informal tones given the connection of such actions toward disrespect (Ford, 2011; Patton & Catching, 2009; Pittman, 2010a). Some signals can help to establish respect. Err on dressing more formally. Create an expectation of being called by honorifics and last names. Arrive in plenty of time to be calm and unrushed. Do not overly share personal information. Focus on being a great teacher and earning respect. Do not try to be a friend.

Communicate expectations in a well-prepared syllabus. Many universities consider the syllabus to be the legal document of a course, including for determining academic violations. Often this critical information is not published anywhere and is part of the unspoken rules of academia that professors should know. If a student is accused of cheating, the language in the syllabus plays a critical role in determining whether the student will be punished. Know what is required for a syllabus at that particular university and include any required language.

OVERCOMING IMPOSTER SYNDROME

Often in the first years of teaching, instructors focus on themselves rather than the students. Research indicates that female faculty spend a great deal more time on their teaching than male faculty, despite knowing the lack of value of teaching in promotion processes (Griffin et al., 2013). Despite similar articulation of expectations, this research reports that female faculty worry more about their teaching and express greater concern about the possibility of negative teaching evaluations.

The irony is that instruction and the student experience can be better when a teacher works less and expects the students to work harder. Shift the gaze to what learning is occurring rather than what teaching is happening. The task is about providing a container in which students work hard.

Slow down. It is possible to be overprepared. It is possible to cover too much content. Often new teachers try to cover too much. Speak slowly.

Allow for wait time. Allow for questions. Check for confusion. Be curious. Embrace inquiry rather than delivering the content. Be prepared to cover less if it means deepening the process of learning. Less is more.

Do not assume that "expert" means knowing everything. When stumped, ask the question back to the class when appropriate to gather answers and responses. Realize also that every instructor makes errors. Do not get defensive. Address the error quickly and move on, with confidence.

Keep a time log of preparation time for teaching. An explicit goal of pre-tenured faculty therefore should be to experiment with how *little* time one can spend preparing for teaching and still teach well. Often, sharing the work of creating a space of learning can help students to be successful rather than shouldering the burden of hours of preparation. More than 2 hours of preparation is too much, according to guidebooks on faculty teaching (Rockquemore & Laszloffy, 2015), and I would argue that even that is too much.

COMPETENCIES OF TEACHING

Beyond addressing inner critics and building confidence, the tools of being a competent and confident teacher can be learned. The resources are numerous and very helpful. Most universities also have personnel assigned to support faculty teaching.

Focus on student understanding. Check in on how students are absorbing the material. Maintain curiosity and respond to questions. Keeping a barometer of student learning can help to stave off stressors that arise from ambiguity. Create a safe space for questions and places students can turn for support if they are not succeeding.

Expect participation. Encourage students to voice their thoughts, questions, and confusion. Place the expectation of engagement in the syllabus and attach points to it. Expect learning through speaking and teaching others. Ask lots of questions of students. Begin with small-scale formats through activities such as paired dialogues or student writing responses to questions on large flipchart paper.

Practice wait time. Count to seven slowly while making eye contact with students before saying anything. If they do not respond, do not let them off the hook. Tell then to turn to a neighbor and answer the question; then bring the group together and post the question again.

Seek out tools and protocols readily available. Collect syllabi from professors at other universities. Drawing upon powerful instructional examples increases the likelihood of energized classroom experiences. Experts in curricular design and pedagogy have developed structures that have been studied to assess the quality of student learning while reducing preparation time. These tools are structured processes designed to improve classroom discussion and deepen learning by using the best of teaching techniques, such as reflection time and active listening (Matoon, 2015). For example, the National School Reform Faculty (NSRF) website offers pages of expert-designed protocols ready for instructor use (National School Reform Faculty, 2019).

Keep detailed lesson plans and records. Design a lecture once and use it for future semesters. Make notes after class about what went well. Tweak for next time rather than starting over.

Build upon the syllabi of others. Design syllabi based on courses colleagues teach at other universities—maybe even courses from your own graduate program. Teach what is familiar and make use of assignments and strategies that have worked well for others. Overemphasize known content and topics that are personally inspiring.

Teach your own research. Get inspired to write and publish by sharing data and drafts of your own writing with students as a part of their learning process—it will deepen understanding for students and also yourself. It may even help you improve your own writing and get past blocks in productivity. Plus, students will also sense your energy when you teach about your passions, and they will feed on that energy.

Invite students to assist with teaching. If you are not provided with a teaching assistant, ask top students if they want credit or the experience of helping the next time. Assign them with the administrative work of a course website, simplified grading, and basic communication with students. Give an assistant the chance to practice running the class on a day—especially on a topic that the student might be familiar with.

Choose guest lectures carefully. Have colleagues visit the class or join virtually from other parts of the world. However, do not invite guest lecturers for the sake of filling time in the syllabus. Guests who do not relate well to course content will create more work, since they create confusion for students and require the instructor to make the connections for them.

As a pre-tenured scholar, José was assigned to teach a large survey course to freshmen and sophomores covering the basic overview of educational foundations. He was advised by colleagues to invite lots of guest lecturers to help fill the year and to reduce his preparation time. The colleagues came, but José found himself struggling to hold the class together, since the guest speakers would lecture on what they wanted to say, and thus created a patchwork of experiences and reflections but no coherent thread that allowed the students to make sense of what educational foundations were.

With so many guest lecturers, José found his lectures trying to tie together disparate ideas rather than creating a cohesive set of content. The students were disgruntled, and his confidence wavered as an instructor. What in the short term seemed to be a time-saving device led to poor student ratings of his teaching and a lack of satisfaction in the experience that he had provided for his students. In future years, José chose guest speakers selectively. This meant he was doing more of the preparation, but the course felt more coherent and he felt more agentic and purposeful as an instructor.

COMPETENCIES OF ONLINE TEACHING

The expectation of teaching online accelerated during the COVID-19 pandemic, and the post-COVID world will keep online teaching as a much larger part of the teaching portfolio of most faculty. Yet research indicates that online programs have historically had much lower student retention than residential programs (Whiteside, Garrett Dikkers, & Lewis, 2014. However, the appeal of online programs continues to grow—to working students, to mothers juggling child care—and otherwise seems to be a sign of what is to come.

Expect interaction and participation online. Create clear expectations for your students—for example, tell them they should log in regularly and ask questions by requiring interaction through the tools provided in the online system. Align grading with responding to one another. Hide requests for participation within recorded material so that students must move through all of the content to complete the work.

Create structures that can run themselves and that require less monitoring. Learn how to give feedback automatically by setting up assessments that offer correct answers and information within the structure of the programming.

Avoid being constantly available. Online teaching does not mean broadening boundaries of availability. Make it clear what days and hours you are available both in the office and online, and stick to that schedule.

Consider the equity issues related to students learning remotely. The learning environments might vary dramatically based on economic and family circumstances. Requiring cameras or microphones to be on may not be the right policy for all students due to shame related to their environment as well as bandwidth issues in areas with little Internet reliability.

COMPETENCIES OF SIMPLIFIED GRADING

Measurement of student progress requires careful planning. Clear expectations up front and examples of quality work can improve student performance (Andrade, 2000). Faculty lose large amounts of time by developing cumbersome grading policies. Creating systems up front can speed up grading over time.

Develop and borrow rubrics. Rubrics can make grading consistent and even reduce student complaints by clearly stating expectations of work quality. Rubrics offer an efficient way to give students the feedback they want in a way that is easy for faculty to deliver. Writing a rubric will also help clarify the intentions for the assignment. Rubrics can also help with timely grading. Students want feedback in a timely enough manner that they know how they are doing in the class. Simple grading processes facilitates returning assignments to students quickly. See Appendix C for a sample rubric.

Grade on content, but do not edit student work. Focus on whether students are meeting the objectives of the class and avoid a focus on grammar if it is not the topic of the course. Send students to campus writing centers if their writing is not up to standard. Focus the most feedback on struggling students.

Divide large assignments into smaller tasks. Just as breaking one's own writing into smaller tasks leads to greater producitivity, students also benefit from larger projects broken into smaller assignments. In addition to reducing stress and improving assignment completion, research indicates that students learn more from frequent, lower-stakes assessment than a few high-stakes assessments (Roediger, Nestojko, & Smith, 2019). Breaking up work—for example, turning a huge research project into smaller assignments—provides students with more formative feedback and improves the quality of their work. It also prevents students from waiting until the end of the semester to ask for help, when it is too late to remediate student procrastination and confusion.

Plagiarism and cheating are increasing. Online assessments and assignments are particularly rife opportunities for cheating, and professors try to avoid these actions through timed assignments (Seltzer, 2015). The design of assessments and grading can help stave off plagiarism, which is a growing problem, according to one study of college presidents (Parker & Lenhart, 2011). Most of the respondents cited computers and the Internet as reasons for the increase in plagiarism. The use of technology makes it much easier to copy and paste the writing of others into papers. Some of this cheating is intentional, and other incidences result from ignorance because students may not understand what plagiarism looks like.

Take time at the beginning of a course to make students familiar with the university's policy on cheating and plagiarism and to create an expectation that they understand what plagiarism is. Know what formal processes exist, whether it be academic integrity committees for cheating or anonymous reporting mechanisms for bias claims.

Danielle administered a midterm for her online course. When grading the midterms, she found that two of her students had submitted the same answers. When she confronted the students, they claimed that they did not understand that midterms were expected to be completed independently, since it was an online assignment. The issue escalated to the college's academic integrity committee, which ruled that the students were correct, since the syllabus did not state the expectation that the assignment was to be completed independently.

In her university, the syllabus is the legal document that determines what assignments count as independent versus group work and can determine when a student is viewed as cheating versus collaborating. Grading scales and deadlines are only as good as the written document. Anything Danielle announced verbally in class would not be upheld in a university hearing if it was not in the written syllabus.

Know the procedures for academic violation before they occur. Organization and careful planning can help you separate student cheating from course disorganization and a lack of clear expectations.

ADDRESSING STRUCTURES THAT REPLICATE BIAS AND DISCRIMINATION

Structures perpetuate inequities within classrooms as much as in broader university contexts. Attending to unspoken rules in classrooms as a teacher includes making biases explicit when they are revealed in student conversations as well. It is important to be ready to address biased comments before they occur. These incidents will include misinformation, microaggressions, and intentional slurs. An ideal process includes an acknowledgment of the problematic nature of the comment or action while not shutting students down in the future who might share similar perspectives. Without opportunities for dialogue, moving the dial on injustice cannot occur.

Research finds that the level of student civility in classrooms is related to the extent to which teachers alienate themselves or build connection (Boice, 2000). Yet even with such efforts, tensions between privileged students and underrepresented faculty may prevent faculty from building such rapport. Strategies for addressing bias in the classroom include the following (adapted from sources including Kardia & Wright, 2004; Seltzer, 2015; and Vargas, 2002):

Let other students respond first. They will be able to say things more directly than the instructor can without shutting down the conversation. However, never expect any student in the class to speak on behalf of a group of students.

Focus on nonreactivity. Breathe. Respond with objectivity rather with accusation.

Connect addressing the comment with the objectives of the course. Explain why students should have an awareness of racial or gender differences if they are interested in these topics.

Be aware that these students may target anger toward faculty who choose to speak about bias and microaggressions. Students uncomfortable with the conversation are apt to call the professor biased (Seltzer, 2015, p. 70; Vargas, 2002). Accusations of bias tend to be much higher for underrepresented faculty, including LGBTQ instructors (Beagan, Mohamed, Brooks, Waterfield, & Weinberg al., 2021) and students (Cech & Rothwell, 2018).

A great deal of research on accusation of bias has examined the experiences of faculty of color. Black women in particular face a greater likelihood of being challenged on whether their expertise qualifies them to teach the course. White students are more likely to complain about Black female teachers to their superiors (Griffin et al., 2013; McGowan, 2000; Pittman, 2010b; Rockquemore & Laszloffy, 2008). Research finds that faculty of color are evaluated more harshly on teacher evaluations. Underrepresented faculty also put more time and effort into teaching to preemptively avoid such negative criticism (Kardia & Wright, 2004; Seltzer, 2015).

Conflicts will arise with students in some fashion for all faculty. A student may disagree with a grading policy. A student may be caught cheating. A student can accuse a faculty member of bias. In all situations, responding without reactivity and gaining broader support is critical. Knowing how to respond before such a situation arises helps faculty stay calm and have clarity on how to proceed.

Involve supportive superiors early. Alert senior-level people early when a potential conflict might be developing and ask for advice on how to deescalate the conflict. These might include a department head, an associate dean for multicultural affairs, or someone from human resources. Ask how they would like you to handle grievances, and maintain regular contact in writing, documenting that you are following the recommended processes.

Do not meet with angry students alone. Bring a supportive colleague to any individual meetings with a student that might involve a conflict. This colleague can serve as a witness to the conversations and also provide you with strategies to deescalate a situation. Follow up any meetings with written documentation about what was discussed. Create a paper trail of the process.

Deal with helicopter parents who demand information. Parents might believe that they have the right to contact professors. Be very clear about the Family Educational Rights and Privacy Act (FERPA) privacy guidelines. It is usually illegal to provide direct information to parents regarding students over the age of 18.

EMPOWERING STUDENTS BY CREATING EQUITABLE CLASSROOM SPACES

By mastering individual skills and addressing inequitable structures, teachers have the opportunity to empower students. It is possible to use the classroom to examine and question spaces of bias. Model a classroom that is inclusive of a range of perspectives and gifts, as well as a place to learn from setbacks. Discuss with students how you think about problems. Share your own struggles and failures as well as successes to model vulnerability as a part of the process of learning.

Teach the content that you wished you had learned. Expose the unspoken rules of succeeding in the academy, much as this book has tried to do. Choose to model safe spaces. Design classrooms in which it feels safe to ask questions and to share messy ideas. Consider ways in which assignments can be constructed that do not create extra burdens for students who might not have broad support networks. The text box offers some ways to reflect on how you might want to explicitly teach about breaking the code of academia with students.

Create a welcoming syllabus. The syllabus is often the students' first interaction with a course. Language signaling a welcoming, inclusive environment will encourage a diverse class. Having an inclusive syllabus that includes objectives and content can inspire students from a range of backgrounds to feel welcome in the classroom and to share their voices and experience. Include information on issues such as disability access and learn where to gather such resources in the syllabus.

> ### JOURNAL QUESTIONS FOR CONNECTING TEACHING
> ### WITH BREAKING THE CODE
>
> - In what ways can you increase student voice and ownership in your classroom?
> - How can you contribute to sharing and teaching the unspoken code of your field and your institution?
> - Where in your curricula do you assume knowledge that students might not know? How can you make it more transparent?
> - What new forms of interaction can you introduce to the classroom space that would encourage students to share questions, embrace vulnerability, and engage with one another?

Share the knowledge generation with students. Structure assignments to have students share in leading the class. Ask students to submit questions for discussion ahead of class. Have students present pieces of the material that you know the least. "Jigsaw" a lesson by breaking the content into smaller parts, and assign groups of students to present a piece of the content to the rest of the class.

Assess the range of perspectives in the classroom. Before engaging in controversial and difficult issues, structure difficult conversations by drawing upon resources for teaching on difficult topics, such as teaching protocols intended to allow a greater understanding of the perspective of the room. Consider how you can make the content more inclusive of a range of perspectives and voices. Seek help on finding resources that support diversity, equity, and inclusion.

Acknowledge privilege. It is the job of faculty to look for bias in unspoken rules across academia. Model the discussion of privilege and the ways in which having privilege grants permission to not engage in discussions of oppression. For example, as a White teacher, it is my obligation to speak of the ways in which I contribute to racism. Rather than choosing to stay silent, I try to embrace discomfort by discussing racial injustice with my students and in my many roles as a teacher and faculty member.

Design the classroom to encourage engagement. For in-person classes, rearrange the physical classroom to encourage dialogue and discussion. The space in a room creates expectations of the power dynamic. When stuck with an auditorium or immovable desks, do not let that space define the room. Collaboration in small groups can still happen across chairs in a lecture hall.

Engagement is also possible in online classes. Use breakout rooms in Zoom and related online platforms. Create interactive quizzes. Schedule group work between classes.

Help students with mental health needs find support. Today's university students need greater support mechanisms than previous generations. The rate of mental health issues of all students, including depression and anxiety, is skyrocketing, and the support services provided by universities are often inadequate. College students have greater levels of stress and psychopathology than any time in history. Anxiety, depression, disordered eating, and learning disabilities are examples. Have clearly stated policies in the syllabus for late work and for what documentation is needed by students when requesting extended time to complete work due to illnesses and emergencies.

Many first-generation students speak of struggling to learn at home with family who do not understand the expectations of a college experience. Some have family members with disabilities or small siblings who disrupt their studying and class-taking. Others lack Internet connection to access online classwork, such as in rural areas. These issues have always existed in universities, but their visibility became more pronounced during the pandemic. Although living on a college campus can help alleviate some of these concerns, doing so does not eliminate the extra jobs that students may need to take on in order to pay their bills (and sometimes to send money home as well).

One semester I had a student who kept falling asleep in my class. I came to find out that he was working an extra job so that his twin brother, an engineer, could study longer. They also were living on the sofas of friends because their substandard housing had a carbon monoxide leak. From a faculty perspective, all I could see without asking was a student who could not stay awake in class. Asking him a question about how he was doing unleashed all of his fears and struggles. I was able to connect him to support services, who found him and his brother a safer apartment, plus an extra loan and grant so that my student could drop his second job. Even with those supports, his lack of a family safety net meant that any crisis threatened his ability to remain in school.

Each semester I find students with similar struggles, and the numbers seem to be increasing.

RECOMMENDATIONS FOR UNIVERSITIES

- Invest in a range of faculty support services to support teaching, including in-person workshops and online tutorial support.
- Provide assistance for online course development. The top universities in the online market offer paid professionals who pair with faculty to develop online content that engages learners.
- Inform faculty early and regularly about the legal aspects of teaching, including how to design a syllabus that conforms with university rules.
- Create a transparent process by which faculty can receive support and guidance when faced with a troubled student.
- Increase support for first-generation college students and underrepresented students, including emergency grant and loan availability and affordable housing.

CHAPTER 10

Conclusion

Creating equitable spaces in which all faculty can thrive demands that universities commit to addressing bias and develop inclusive structures and cultures. This book demonstrated how a coaching-focused stance toward faculty development can contribute to faculty retention and improved well-being. By speaking to both faculty and universities, I focused on the ways in which structure and agency combine to improve the lived experiences of faculty members. Institutional structures inhibit success when they do not attend to policies that discourage bias, inequity, and obfuscation. By looking at both structures and individual development, this book offered a pathway to faculty success.

The book highlighted the need for faculty to include a strong foundation of equity, and for universities to consider how inclusive and transparent their administrative policies are. By developing personalized support for faculty, including one-on-one coaching strategies and cohort-style support for pre-tenured and mid-career faculty, universities have the potential to retain a diverse faculty who are thriving and active members of the university community. A coaching stance can especially help universities provide support for faculty struggling to make adequate progress toward their next promotions, as well as proactively construct ongoing professional learning opportunities to promote a healthy culture for all faculty to improve retention and to increase faculty fulfillment across their careers.

Faculty development can improve through discussions of unspoken rules, transparency, and bias. Faculty should have opportunities to assess climate and to discuss the findings and participate in creating strategic plans to address these issues. This book addressed the need to make institutional structures explicit. Through discussions of unspoken norms, implicit bias becomes a focus of conversations. The book also provided strategies for faculty to see the implicit and explicit inequities in their lived experience and explored how norms can become embedded within individuals as inner critics. These voices can impede careers and stop productivity by infusing doubt and imposter syndrome into the minds of academics.

The book also demonstrated the ways in which faculty members must understand themselves and the structures in which they work—the places where they currently work and potential places of employment. These processes include deciding when to remain at an institution and find greater satisfaction. Success also may mean choosing to challenge an institution or to shift to a university that is a better fit. The book has interwoven coaching-focused chapters with the traditional components of the academic structure—research, service, and teaching—to show how to make each aspect of one's career more intentional and purpose-driven. The ABC Framework illustrated the fundamental building blocks for faculty fulfillment: developing *agency* provides the foundation of a solid academic experience through intentional tethering of purpose and values; making strategic choices in *belonging* to networks and communities creates a web of support; and mastering the necessary *competencies* reduces background stressors and improves goal setting. A fulfilled career depends on learning how to keep tethered to one's purpose while finding ways to navigate institutional structures.

List of Core Values

Ability	Carefulness	Curiosity
Abundance	Certainty	Daring
Acceptance	Challenge	Decisiveness
Accomplishment	Charity	Decorum
Achievement	Charm	Deepness
Adaptability	Chastity	Delicacy
Adventure	Cheerfulness	Delight
Affection	Clarity	Dependability
Affluence	Classy	Depth
Alertness	Cleverness	Desire
Ambition	Closeness	Determination
Anticipation	Comfort	Devotion
Appreciation	Commitment	Dexterity
Approachability	Compassion	Dignity
Artfulness	Competence	Diligence
Assertiveness	Completion	Diplomacy
Assurance	Composure	Direction
Attentiveness	Concentration	Directness
Audacity	Confidence	Discernment
Availability	Conformity	Discipline
Awareness	Congruency	Discovery
Awe	Connection	Discretion
Balance	Consciousness	Diversity
Beauty	Consistency	Dreaming
Being-ness	Contentment	Drive
Belongingness	Continuity	Dynamism
Benevolence	Contribution	Eagerness
Blissfulness	Control	Economy
Boldness	Conviction	Ecstasy
Bravery	Conviviality	Education
Brilliance	Cooperation	Effectiveness
Buoyancy	Copiousness	Efficiency
Calmness	Correctness	Elation
Camaraderie	Courage	Elegance
Candor	Courtesy	Empathy
Capability	Creativity	Encouragement
Care	Credibility	Endurance

Energy	Harmony	Mindfulness
Enjoyment	Health	Moderation
Enlightenment	Heart	Modesty
Entertainment	Helpfulness	Motivation
Enthusiasm	Heroism	Mysteriousness
Evolution	Holiness	Neatness
Excellence	Honesty	Nerve
Excitement	Honor	Obedience
Exhilaration	Hopefulness	Open-mindedness
Expectancy	Humility	Openness
Expediency	Humor	Optimism
Experience	Imagination	Opulence
Expertise	Impact	Order
Exploration	Impeccability	Organization
Extravagance	Independence	Originality
Exuberance	Ingenuity	Outlandishness
Facilitating	Inquisitiveness	Outrageousness
Fairness	Insightfulness	Passion
Faith	Inspiration	Peacefulness
Fame	Instinctiveness	Perceptiveness
Fearlessness	Integrity	Perfection
Fidelity	Intelligence	Perseverance
Finesse	Intensity	Persistence
Firmness	Intimacy	Persuasiveness
Fitness	Intrepidness	Philanthropy
Flexibility	Introversion	Piety
Flow	Intuition	Playfulness
Fluency	Intuitiveness	Pleasantness
Fluidity	Inventiveness	Pleasure
Focus	Joy	Plentiful-ness
Fortitude	Judiciousness	Poise
Frankness	Justice	Polish
Freedom	Kindness	Popularity
Friendliness	Leadership	Practicality
Frugality	Learning	Pragmatism
Fun	Liberation	Precision
Generosity	Liberty	Preeminence
Gentility	Liveliness	Preparedness
Genuineness	Logic	Presence
Giving	Longevity	Privacy
Grace	Love	Proactivity
Gratefulness	Loyalty	Professionalism
Gratitude	Majesty	Proficiency
Gregariousness	Mastery	Prosperity
Growth	Maturity	Prudence
Guidance	Mellowness	Purity
Happiness	Meticulousness	Qualification

Quickness
Quietness
Readiness
Realism
Reason
Recognition
Refinement
Reflection
Reliability
Resilience
Resolution
Resolve
Resourcefulness
Respect
Restfulness
Reverence
Richness
Rigor
Sacredness
Sacrifice
Sagacity
Saintliness
Sanguinity
Satisfaction
Security
Self-control
Selflessness
Self-realization
Self-reliance

Sensitivity
Sensuality
Serenity
Service
Sharing
Shrewdness
Significance
Simplicity
Sincerity
Skillfulness
Solidarity
Solidity
Solitude
Sophistication
Soundness
Speed
Spirit
Spirituality
Spontaneity
Stability
Stillness
Strength
Structure
Substantiality
Success
Sufficiency
Superb
Support
Supremacy

Surprise
Sympathy
Synergy
Tactfulness
Teamwork
Temperance
Thankfulness
Thoroughness
Thoughtfulness
Thrift
Timeliness
Traditionalism
Tranquility
Transcendence
Trustworthiness
Truth
Uniqueness
Unity
Utility
Valor
Victory
Vigor
Vision
Vitality
Warmth
Watchfulness
Wonder

(Content Sparks, 2019)

My Strategic Plan, 2017–2018

Goal 1: Submit mindfulness paper

- P1. Read models on principalship
  - Read various models on principal standards
  - Check and create model
  - Check expectations on = standards
- P2. Data
  - Connect models together
  - Read literature on principalship and mindfulness
  - Create model for principal competencies
- P3. Write
  - Introduction
  - Literature
  - Principal standards
  - Mindfulness model
  - My model
  - Conclusion
- P4. Revising
  - Revise paper
  - Revise literature review
  - Revise model
  - Revise discussion
  - Send to Deb for review
  - Revise based on her comments
  - Search for fit journal
  - Submit to journal

Goal 2: Submit stressors paper

- P1. Finalize findings
  - Pull out main findings from dissertation
  - Pull out methodology from dissertation
  - Pull out literature from dissertation

- Pull out discussion from dissertation
- Write introduction
- P2. Read sample papers
  - Check journals suitable for such paper
  - Collect additional articles and literature
  - Combine all parts for paper
- P3. Revise
  - Send to D for review
  - Revise based on D comments
  - Revise introduction
  - Revise discussion
  - Write cover letter
  - Submit to journal

Goal 3: Submit outcomes paper

- P1. Finalize findings
  - Pull out main findings from dissertation
  - Pull out methodology from dissertation
  - Pull out literature from dissertation
  - Pull out discussion from dissertation
  - Write introduction
- P2. Read sample papers
  - Check journals suitable for such paper
  - Collect additional articles and literature
  - Combine all parts for paper
- P3. Revise
  - Send to D for review
  - Revise based on D comments
  - Revise introduction
  - Revise discussion
  - Write cover letter
  - Submit to journal

Goal 4: Submit Receptivity paper

- P1. Read sample papers
  - Check journals suitable for such paper
  - Outline paper
- P2. Read & collect papers on receptivity
  - Reach out to Rob on receptivity
  - Reach out to Greenberg
  - Collect literature on receptivity

- Collect literature on principalship and identity
- Collect data on mindfulness
- P3. Literature & Methodology
  - Pull out methodology from dissertation
  - Outline literature review
- P4. Data
  - Pull out data from dissertation
  - Outline the findings
- P5. Write (12/9/16)
  - Introduction
  - Literature
  - Methodology
  - Findings
  - Discussion
  - Conclusion
- P6. Revise
  - Revise paper
  - Revise literature review
  - Send Rob and Greenberg paper for revision
  - Revise based on their comments
  - Prepare draft for submission
  - Search suitable journal
  - Submit to journal

Week	Mondays	Notes	Research	Personal
2	9/4		TAMAM P1 & P2 Mindfulness 1 P1	Exercise 3x/week 2–4-mile run Read 2x a week Mindfulness 5x Spend time with family Talk to friends
3	9/11	Teaching Prep		Exercise 3x/week 2–4-mile run Read 2x a week Mindfulness 5x Spend time with family Talk to friends
4	9/18		Goal 4	Exercise 3x/week 2–4-mile run Read 2x a week

Week	Mondays	Notes	Research	Personal
				Mindfulness 5x
				Spend time with family
				Talk to friends
5	9/25		Goal 1	Exercise 3x/week
				2–4-mile run
				Read 2x a week
				Mindfulness 5x
				Spend time with family
				Talk to friends
6	10/2		Goal 3	Exercise 3x/week
				2–4-mile run
				Read 2x a week
				Mindfulness 5x
				Spend time with family
				Talk to friends
7	10/9	Mindfulness Retreat [12–15]	Goal 2	Exercise 3x/week
				2–4-mile run
				Read 2x a week
				Mindfulness 5x
				Spend time with family
				Talk to friends
8	10/16			Exercise 3x/week
				2–4-mile run
				Read 2x a week
				Mindfulness 5x
				Spend time with family
				Talk to friends
9	10/23			Exercise 3x/week
				2–4-mile run
				Read 2x a week
				Mindfulness 5x
				Spend time with family
				Talk to friends

Sample Paper Rubric

Name:

	Insufficient—C	Adequate—B	Excellent—A
Evaluation: Strengths and weaknesses	• Cursory list of strengths and weaknesses. • No outside evidence provided; opinion given instead of analysis.	• Some strengths and weaknesses given. • Writing is somewhat disjointed. • Statements attempt to incorporate concepts from class and outside evidence. • Some components may appear "off the top of the head."	• Coherent discussion of the policy. • Strengths and weaknesses flow well together to create a unified analysis of many aspects of the policy. • Effective use of outside information and references to strengthen argument.
Final recommendation	• Final recommendation missing.	• Final recommendation included but cursory or does not build off analysis.	• Final recommendation is a sophisticated conclusion building on evidence and analysis from the paper.
Overall mastery of subject matter	• Student appears to not have a complete grasp of their policy topic.	• Paper answers the questions in the assignment yet does so in a disjointed manner.	• Evidence of extra effort given to understand their topic, including seeking out evidence from others.

	Insufficient—C	Adequate—B	Excellent—A
	• No reference to course material.	• Paper makes reference to concepts discussed in class. • Adequate mastery of subject matter, yet some nuances are missing.	• Solid mastery of class readings and discussions demonstrated.
Flow of paper	• Writing is disjointed. • Paper lacks some basic components of college writing, such as no bibliography, lack of paragraphs, serious grammatical errors, etc. • Paper is missing sections. • Paper does not use APA style.	• Paper is written with a few errors of technical writing skills, including grammar, using paragraphs, subheadings, and correct citations. • Paper is overall cursory and lacking in full description for the sections. • Paper has references but not enough peer-reviewed evidence. • Subheaders confusing or too many. • Paper uses APA style incorrectly.	• Strong writing style that coherently connects ideas and builds an argument throughout the paper. • Strong technical writing skills, including subheaders for rubric sections and page numbers. • Solid mastery of topic sources. • Paper is well organized, including subheadings that clearly delineate the sections of the paper. • Paper includes at least 3 peer-reviewed citations, and these citations are incorporated as evidence in the paper. • Paper uses APA style correctly.

OVERALL GRADE:

References

Ambrose, S., Huston, T., & Norman, M. (2005). A qualitative method for assessing faculty satisfaction. *Research in Higher Education*, 46(7), 803–830.

American Council on Education. (2001). *A brief guide to U.S. higher education*. Washington, DC: American Council on Education.

Amey, M. J. (1996). The institutional marketplace and faculty attrition. *Thought and Action*, XII, 23–36.

Andrade, H. G. (2000). Using rubrics to promote thinking and learning. *Educational Leadership*, 57(5), 13–19.

Antonio, A. L. (2003). Diverse student bodies, diverse faculties. *Academe*, 89(6), 14.

August, L., & Waltman, J. (2004). Culture, climate, and contribution: Career satisfaction among female faculty. *Research in Higher Education*, 45(2), 177–192.

Austin, A. E., Sorcinelli, M. D., & McDaniels, M. (2007). Understanding new faculty: Background, aspirations, challenges, and growth. In R. P. Perry & J. C. Smart (Eds.), *The scholarship of teaching and learning in higher education: An evidence-based perspective* (pp. 39–89). Springer.

Baez, B. (2000). Race-related service and faculty of color: Conceptualizing critical agency in academe. *Higher Education*, 39, 363–391.

Bandura, A. (2000). Exercise of human agency through collective efficacy. *Current Directions in Psychological Science*, 9(3), 75–78.

Barley, S. R., & Tolbert, P. S. (1997). Institutionalization and structuration: Studying the links between action and institution. *Organization Studies*, 18(1), 93–117.

Barlett, P. F., & Rappaport, A. (2009). Long-term impacts of faculty development programs: The experience of Teli and Piedmont. *College Teaching*, 57(2), 73–82.

Barnes, K. Y., & Mertz, E. E. (2010). Is it fair? Law professors' perceptions of tenure. *Journal of Legal Education*, 61(4), Arizona Legal Studies Discussion Paper No. 10-44, American Bar Foundation Research Paper No. 11-02.

Bauer, T. N., Bodner, T., Erdogan, B., Truxillo, D. M., & Tucker, J. S. (2007). Newcomer adjustment during organizational socialization: A meta-analytic review of antecedents, outcomes, and methods. *Journal of Applied Psychology*, 92(3), 707–721.

Bavishi, A., Madera, J. M., & Hebl, M. R. (2010). The effect of professor ethnicity and gender on student evaluations: Judged before met. *Journal of Diversity in Higher Education*, 3(4), 245–256. http://www.depts.ttu.edu/diversity/ccaac/bavishi-article.pdf.

Beagan, B. L., Mohamed, T., Brooks, K., Waterfield, B., & Weinberg, M. (2021). Microaggressions experienced by LGBTQ academics in Canada: "Just not fitting in . . . it does take a toll." *International Journal of Qualitative Studies in Education, 34*(3), 197–212.

Bilimoria, D., Joy, S., & Liang, X. (2008). Breaking barriers and creating inclusiveness: Lessons of organizational transformation to advance women faculty in academic science and engineering. *Human Resource Management, 47*(3), 423–441.

Bird, S. (2011). Unsettling universities' incongruous, gendered bureaucratic structures: A case-study approach. *Gender, Work and Organization, 18*(2), 202–230.

Blackburn, R. T., & Lawrence, J. H. (1995). *Faculty at work: Motivation, expectation, satisfaction.* Johns Hopkins University Press.

Blanchard, K. (2012, January 31). I've got tenure. How depressing. *Chronicle of Higher Education.* https://www.chronicle.com/article/Ive-Got-Tenure-How /130490

Boice, R. (2000). *Advice for new faculty members: Nihil nimus.* Allyn & Bacon.

Bolker, J. (1998). *Writing your dissertation in fifteen minutes a day: A guide to starting, revising, and finishing your doctoral thesis.* Holt Paperbacks.

Bova, B., & Kroth, M. (2001). Workplace learning and Generation X. *Journal of Workplace Learning, 13*(2), 57–65.

Boyd, T., Cintrón, R., & Alexander-Snow, M. (2010). The experience of being a junior minority female faculty member. *Oxford Round Table, Forum on Public Policy Online, 2010*(2).

Brach, T. (2019). *Radical compassion: Learning to love yourself and our work with the practice of RAIN.* Viking Press.

Brown, B. (2010). *The gifts of imperfection: Let go of who you think you're supposed to be and embrace who you are.* Hazelden Publishing.

Brown, B. (2015). *Daring greatly: How the courage to be vulnerable transforms the way we live, love, parent, and lead.* Penguin.

Brown, B. (2017). *Braving the wilderness: The quest for true belonging and the courage to stand alone.* Random House.

Brown, B. (2018). *Dare to lead: Brave work. Tough conversations. Whole hearts.* Random House.

Butner, B. K., Burley, H., & Marbley, A. F. (2000). Coping with the unexpected: Black faculty at predominantly White institutions. *Journal of Black Studies, 30*(3), 453–462.

Cacioppo, J., & Cacioppo, S. (2017). The social muscle. *Harvard Business Review, 10.* https://hbr.org/2017/10/the-social-muscle.

Cacioppo, J. T., & Patrick, W. (2008). *Loneliness: Human nature and the need for social connection.* W. W. Norton & Company.

Cameron, T., & Hyer, P. (2010). *An examination of departure trends and tenure rates among pre-tenured faculty: A ten-year cohort study (1996–2005).* Virginia Tech University

Carrigan, C., Quinn, K., & Riskin, E. A. (2011). The gendered division of labor among STEM faculty and the effects of the critical mass. *Journal of Diversity in Higher Education, 4*(3), 131–146.

Cawyer, C. S., & Friedrich, G. W. (1998). Organizational socialization: Processes for new communication faculty. *Communication Education, 47,* 234–245.

Cech, E. A., & Rothwell, W. R. (2018). LGBTQ inequality in engineering education. *Journal of Engineering Education, 107*(4), 583–610.

Childre, A., Sands, J. R., & Pope, S. T. (2009). Backward design. *Teaching Exceptional Children, 41*(5), 6–14.

Clark, A., & Sousa, B. (2018). *How to be a happy academic: A guide to being effective in research, writing and teaching*. Sage.

Colbeck, C. L., & Wharton-Michael, P. (2006). Individual and organizational influences on faculty members' engagement in public scholarship. *New Directions for Teaching and Learning, 2006*(105), 17–26.

Collaborative on Academic Careers in Higher Education. (2007). *COACHE Highlights Report 2007*. http://www.users.miamioh.edu/shorec/apapff/resources/COACHE_ReportHighlights_20070801.pdf

Collins, R. (2004). *Interactional ritual chain*. Princeton University Press.

Content Sparks. (2019). Big list of value words. https://contentsparks.com/16896/free-download-big-list-of-core-value-words/

Costello, J., Toles, M., Spielberger, J., & Wynn, J. (2000). History, ideology and structure shape the organizations that shape youth. In N. Jaffe, (Ed.), *Youth development: Issues, challenges, and directions* (pp. 185–231). Public/Private Ventures.

Crenshaw, K. W. (2017). *On intersectionality: Essential writings*. New Press.

Daley, S., Wingard, D. L., & Reznik, V. (2006). Improving the retention of underrepresented minority faculty in academic medicine. *Journal of the National Medical Association, 98*(9), 1435–1440.

Deci, E. L., & Ryan, R. M. (2000). The "what" and "why" of goal pursuits: Human needs and the self-determination of behavior. *Psychological Inquiry, 11*(4), 227–268.

Delgado, R., & Stefanick, J. (2017). *Critical race theory: An introduction*. New York University Press.

Denson, N., Szelényi, K., & Bresonis, K. (2018). Correlates of work-life balance for faculty across racial/ethnic groups. *Research in Higher Education, 59*(2), 226–247.

Diaz, V., Garrett, P. B., Kinley, E, Moore, J., & Schwartz, C. (2009). Faculty development for the 21st century. *EDUCAUSE Review, 44*(3), 46–55.

Diggs, G. A., Garrison-Wade, D. F., Estrada, D., & Galindo, R. (2009). Smiling faces and colored spaces: The experiences of faculty of color pursuing tenure in the academy. *The Urban Review, 41*(4), 312–333.

Dooris, M., & Guidos, M. (2006, May). Tenure achievement rates at research universities [Paper presentation]. Annual Forum of the Association for Institutional Research, Chicago, IL.

Drago, R., & Colbeck, C. (2003). Final report from the mapping project: Exploring the terrain of US colleges and universities for faculty and families. Pennsylvania State University.

Drennan, J., Clarke, M., Hyde, A., & Politis, Y. (2013). The research function of the academic profession in Europe. In U. Teichler & E. A. Höhle (Eds.), *The work situation of the academic profession in Europe: Findings of a survey in twelve countries* (pp. 109–136). Springer.

Dutton, J. E. (2003). *Energize your workplace: How to build and sustain high-quality connections at work*. Jossey-Bass Publishers.

Dutton, J. E., & Heaphy, E. D. (2003). The power of high-quality connections. In K. S. Cameron, J. E. Dutton, & R. E. Quinn (Eds.), *Positive organizational scholarship: Foundations of a new discipline* (pp. 262–278). Berrett-Koehler.

Dweck, C. S. (2007). The perils and promises of praise. *Education Leadership*, 65(2), 34–39.

Dweck, C. S. (2010). Mind-sets and equitable education. *Principal Leadership*, 10(5), 26–29.

Eccles, J., & Gootman, J. A. (2002). Community programs to promote youth development. Committee on Community-Level Programs for Youth. Board on Children, Youth, and Families, Commission on Behavioral and Social Sciences Education, National Research Council and Institute of Medicine. National Academies of Science.

Eccles, J. S., Midgley, C., Wigfield, A., Buchanan, C. M., Reuman, D., Flanagan, C., & MacIver, D. (1993). Development during adolescence: The impact of stage-environment fit on young adolescents' experiences in schools and in families. *American Psychologist, 48*(2), 90–101.

Elder, R. W. (1997). An executive's guide to implementing instructional technology in institutions of higher education. George Mason University.

Entis, L. (2016, June 22). Chronic loneliness is a modern-day epidemic. Fortune.com. https://fortune.com/2016/06/22/loneliness-is-a-modern-day-epidemic/

Exum, W. H., Menges, R. J., Watkins, B., & Berglund, P. (1984). Making it at the top: Women and minority faculty in the American labor market. *American Behavioral Scientist, 27*(3), 301–324.

Ford, K. A. (2011). Race, gender, and bodily (mis)recognitions: Women of color faculty experiences with White students in the college classroom. *Journal of Higher Education, 82*(4), 444–478.

Fries-Britt, S., & Kelly, B. T. (2005). Retaining each other: Narratives of two African American women in the academy. *Urban Review, 37*(3), 221–242.

Fries-Britt, S., & Snider, J. (2015). Mentoring outside the line: The importance of authenticity, transparency, and vulnerability in effective mentoring relationships. *New Directions for Higher Education, 2015*(171), 3–11.

Fritz, C., Lam, C. F., & Spreitzer, G. M. (2011). It's the little things that matter: An examination of knowledge workers' energy management. *Academy of Management Perspectives, 25*(3), 28–39.

Galinsky, E., Sakai, K., & Wigton, T. (2011). Workplace flexibility: From research to action. *The Future of Children, 21*(2), 141–161.

Gappa, J. M., Austin, A. E., & Trice, A. G. (2007). *Rethinking faculty work: Higher education's strategic imperative.* Jossey-Bass.

Gardner, S. K. (2013). Women faculty departures from a striving institution: Between a rock and a hard place. *The Review of Higher Education, 36*(3), 349–370.

Garrison-Wade, D., Diggs, D., Estrada, D., & Galindo, R. (2012). Lift every voice and sing: Faculty of color reflections on diversity and equity efforts. *Urban Review, 44*, 1, 90–112.

Giddens, A. (1984). *The constitution of society: Outline of the theory of structuration.* University of California Press.

Gillespie, K. J., & Robertson, D. L. (2010). *A guide to faculty development.* John Wiley & Son.

Gmelch, W., & Schuh, J. H. (2004). *The life cycle of a department chair. New directions for higher education.* Jossey-Bass.

Gonzales, L. D., & Rincones, R. (2012). Interdisciplinary scholars: Negotiating legitimacy at the core and from the margins. *Journal of Further and Higher Education, 36*, 495–518.

Goodenow, C. (1993). Classroom belonging among early adolescent students: Relationship to motivation and achievement. *Journal of Early Adolescence, 13*(1), 21–43.

Greene, J., Stockard, J., Lewis, P., & Richmond, G. (2010). Is the academic climate chilly? The view of women academic chemists. *Journal of Chemical Education, 87*(4), 381–385.

Griffin, K. A. (2020). Institutional barriers, strategies, and benefits to increasing the representation of women and men of color in the professoriate: Looking beyond the pipeline. In L. Pernal, (Ed.), *Higher education: Handbook of theory and research: Volume 35* (pp. 1–73). Springer.

Griffin, K. A., Bennett, J. C., & Harris, J. (2013). Marginalizing merit? Gender differences in Black faculty D/discourses on tenure, advancement, and professional success. *Review of Higher Education, 36*(4), 489–512.

Griffin, K. A., Pifer, M. J., Humphrey, J. R., & Hazelwood, A. M. (2011). (Re) defining departure: Exploring Black professors' experiences with and responses to racism and racial climate. *American Journal of Education, 117*(4), 495–526.

Griffin, K. A., & Reddick, R. J. (2011). Surveillance and sacrifice: Gender differences in the mentoring patterns of Black professors at predominantly White research universities. *American Educational Research Journal, 48*(5), 1032–1057.

Grover, S., & Furnham, A. (2016). Coaching as a developmental intervention in organisations: A systematic review of its effectiveness and the mechanisms underlying it. *PloS one, 11*(7), e0159137.

Gutiérrez y Muhs, G., Niemann, Y. F., González, C. G., & Harris, A. P. (2012). *Presumed incompetent: The intersections of race and class for women in academia.* Utah State Press.

Hagedorn, L. S. (2000). What contributes to job satisfaction among faculty and staff? *New Directions for Institutional Research, 105* (J-B IR Single Issue Institutional Research). Jossey-Bass.

Hanasono, L. K., Broido, E. M., Yacobucci, M. M., Root, K. V., Peña, S., & O'Neil, D. A. (2019). Secret service: Revealing gender biases in the visibility and value of faculty service. *Journal of Diversity in Higher Education, 12*(1), 85–98.

Hansman, C., & McAtee, K. (2014). Faculty development opportunities: Peer coaching, learning communities, and mentoring. *Journal of Education & Human Development, 3*(1), 71–84.

Haras, C. (2018, January 17). Faculty development as an authentic professional practice. *Higher Education Today.* https://www.higheredtoday.org/2018/01/17/faculty-development-authentic-professional-practice/

Herrera, T. (2020, January 5). Thinking about a job or career change? Read this. *New York Times.* https://www.nytimes.com/2020/01/05/smarter-living/thinking-about-a-job-or-career-change-read-this.html?smid=nytcore-ios-share

Hogan, K. (2010, January 8). Managing service duties. *Inside Higher Ed: Career Advice.* https://www.insidehighered.com/advice/2010/01/08/managing-service-duties.

Huston, T., Norman, M., & Ambrose, S. (2007). Expanding the discussion of faculty vitality to include productive but disengaged senior faculty. *Journal of Higher Education, 78*(5), 493–522.

Hyun, J. (2005). *Breaking the bamboo ceiling: Career strategies for Asians.* Harper Business.

James, R. (2014). *Tenure hacks: The 12 secrets of making tenure.* CreateSpace Independent Publishing Platform.

Jayakumar, U., Howard, T. C., Allen, W. R., & Han, J. S. (2009). Racial privilege in the professoriate: An exploration of campus climate, retention, and satisfaction. *Journal of Higher Education, 80*(5), 538–563.

Johnsrud, L. K., & Sadao, K. C. (1998). The common experience of "Otherness": Ethnic and racial minority faculty. *Review of Higher Education, 21*(4), 315–342.

Kamler, B., & Thomson, P. (2014). *Helping doctoral students write: Pedagogies for supervision.* Routledge.

Kardia, D., & Wright, M. (2004). Instructor identity: The impact of gender and race on faculty experiences with teaching. University of Michigan Center for Research on Learning and Teaching (Occasional Paper No. 19).

Kelly, B. T., & Fetridge, J. S. (2012). The role of students in the experience of women faculty on the tenure track. *NASPA Journal About Women in Higher Education, 5*(1), 22–45.

Kelly, B. T., & McCann, K. I. (2014). Women faculty of color: Stories behind the statistics. *Urban Review, 46*(4), 681–702.

Kelly, B. T., & Winkle-Wagner, R. (2017). Finding a voice in predominantly White institutions: A longitudinal study of Black women faculty members' journeys toward tenure. *Teachers College Record, 119*(June), 1–36.

Kimsey-House, H., Kimsey-House, K., Sandahl, P., & Whitworth, L. (2018). *Co-active coaching: Changing business, transforming lives.* Hachette UK.

Kulis, S., Sicotte, D., & Collins, S. (2002). More than a pipeline problem: Labor supply constraints and gender stratification across academic science disciplines. *Research in Higher Education, 43*(6), 657–691.

Ladson-Billings, G., & Tate, W. (1995). Toward a critical race theory of education. *Teachers College Record, 97*(1), 47–64.

Lamott, A. (2007). *Bird by bird: Some instructions on writing and life.* Anchor.

Lander, K. (2019, September 9). Introvert? You may just be bad at recognizing faces. *The Conversation.* https://theconversation.com/introvert-you-may-just-be-bad-at-recognising-faces-123205

Lattuca, L. R. (2001). *Creating interdisciplinarity: Interdisciplinary research and teaching among college and university faculty.* Vanderbilt University Press.

Lawrence, J. H., Celis, S., & Ott, M. (2014). Is the tenure process fair? What faculty think. *Journal of Higher Education, 85*(2), 155–188.

Leather, P., Pyrgas, M., Beale, D., & Lawrence, C. (1998). Windows in the workplace: Sunlight, view, and occupational stress. *Environment and Behavior, 30*(6), 739–762.

Lerner, R. M., Bowers, E. P., Geldhof, G. J., Gestsdóttir, S., & DeSouza, L. (2012). Promoting positive youth development in the face of contextual change and challenges: The roles of individual strengths and ecological assets. *New Directions for Youth Development, 135*, 119–128.

Lewis, P., & Richmond, G. (2010). Women academic chemists. *Journal of Chemical Education, 87*(4), 381–385.

Lewis, P., & Simpson, R. (2012). Kanter revisited: Gender, power and (in) visibility. *International Journal of Management Reviews, 14*(2), 141–158.

Li, J., Tian, M., Fang, H., Xu, M., Li, H., & Liu, J. (2010). Extraversion predicts individual differences in face recognition. *Communicative & Integrative Biology, 3*(4), 295–298.

Link, A. N., Swan, C. A., & Bozeman, B. (2008). A time allocation study of university faculty. *Economics of Education Review, 27*(4), 363–374.

Lochmiller, C. R. (2014). Leadership coaching in an induction program for novice principals: A 3-year study. *Journal of Research on Leadership Education, 9*(1), 59–84.

Louis, R. P. (2007). Can you hear us now? Voices from the margin: Using indigenous methodologies in geographic research. *Geographical Research, 45*(2), 130–139.

Lynton, E. (1995). *Making the case for professional service.* American Association for Higher Education.

Marschke, R., Laursen, S., Nielsen, J. M., & Dunn-Rankin, P. (2007). Demographic inertia revisited: An immodest proposal to achieve equitable gender representation among faculty in higher education. *Journal of Higher Education, 78*(1), 1–26. http://www.jstor.org/stable/4122353

Martin, N. T. (2007). Immunity for hire: How the same-actor doctrine sustains discrimination in the contemporary workplace. *Connecticut Law Review, 40,* 1117.

Mason, M. A., & Goulden, M. (2004, November). Marriage and baby blues: Redefining gender equity in the academy. *Annals of the American Academy of Political and Social Science, 596,* 86–103.

Mason, M. A., Goulden, M., & Frasch, K. (2009). Why graduate students reject the fast track. *Academe, 95*(1), 11–16.

Mathews, K. (2014). *Perspectives on midcareer faculty and advice for supporting them.* Collaborative on Academic Careers in Higher Education. http://coache.gse.harvard.edu/files/gse-coache/files/coache-perspectives-on.pdf?m=1447625224

Matoon, M. (2015). *What are protocols? Why use them?* National School Reform Faculty [NSRF]. https://www.nsrfharmony.org/wp-content/uploads/2017/10/WhatAreProtocolsWhyUse_0.pdf

Matthew, P. A. (Ed.). (2016). *Written/unwritten: Diversity and the hidden truths of tenure.* University of North Carolina Press Books.

McGowan, J. M. (2000). African-American faculty classroom teaching experiences in predominantly White colleges and universities. *Multicultural Education, 8*(2), 19–22.

McKay, N. Y. (1997). A troubled peace: Black women in the halls of the White academy. In Benjamin, L. (Ed.), *Black women in the academy: Promises and perils* (pp. 11–22). University Press of Florida.

Medd, E. L. (2002). *The effects of facilitated incubation on fourth graders' creative writing.* Fordham University.

Menakem, R. (2017). *My grandmother's hands: Racialized trauma and the pathway to mending our hearts and bodies.* Central Recovery Press.

Meyer, J. W., & Rowan, B. (1977). Institutionalized organizations: Formal structure as myth and ceremony. *American Journal of Sociology, 83*(2), 340–363.

Miller, R. A., Guida, T., Smith, S., Ferguson, S. K., & Medina, E. (2018). A balancing act: Whose interests do bias response teams serve? *Review of Higher Education, 42*(1), 313–337.

Misra, J., Lundquist, J., Holmes, E., & Agiomavritis, J. (2011). The ivory ceiling of service work. *Academe, 97*(1), 22–28.

Misra, J., Lundquist, J. H., & Templer, A. (2012,). Gender, work time, and care responsibilities among faculty. *Sociological Forum, 27*(2), 300–323.

Mitchell, S. M., & Hesli, V. L. (2013). Women don't ask? Women don't say no? Bargaining and service in the political science profession. *PS: Political Science & Politics, 46*(2), 355–369.

Mitra, D. L. (2004). The significance of students: Can increasing "student voice" in schools lead to gains in youth development? *Teachers College Record, 106*(4), 651–688.

Mitra, D. L. (2008). Balancing power in communities of practice: An examination of increasing student voice through school-based youth-adult partnerships. *Journal of Educational Change, 9*(3), 221–324.

Mitra, D., & Serriere, S. (2012). Student voice in elementary-school reform: Examining youth development in fifth graders. *American Educational Research Journal, 49*, 743–.

Mohr, T. (2015). *Playing big: Find your voice, your mission, your message.* Avery.

Moore, H. A., Acosta, K., Perry, G., & Edwards, C. (2010). Splitting the academy: The emotions of intersectionality at work. *Sociological Quarterly, 51*, 179–204. doi:10.1111/j.1533-8525.2010. 01168.x.

Morgenstern, J. (2004a). *Time management from the inside out: The foolproof system for taking control of your schedule—and your life.* Holt Paperbacks.

Morgenstern, J. (2004b). *Making work work: New strategies for surviving and thriving at the office.* Simon and Schuster.

Morgenstern, J. (2011). *Never check e-mail in the morning: And other unexpected strategies for making your work life work.* Simon and Schuster.

Museus, S. D., Maramba, D. C., & Teranishi, R. T. (Eds.). (2013). *The misrepresented minority: New insights on Asian Americans and Pacific Islanders, and the implications for higher education.* Stylus Publishing, LLC.

Nagoski, E., & Nagoski, A. (2020). *Burnout: The secret to unlocking the stress cycle.* Ballantine Books.

Nakamura, J., & Csikszentmihalyi, M. (2014). The concept of flow. In M. Csikszentmihalyi, (Ed.), *Flow and the foundations of positive psychology* (pp. 239–263). Springer.

National School Reform Faculty. (2019). *NSRF protocols and activities.* https://www.nsrfharmony.org/protocols/

Neumann, A. (2009). *Professing to learn: Creating tenured lives and careers in the American research university.* Johns Hopkins University Press.

Neumann, A., Terosky, A. L., & Schell, J. (2006). Agents of learning: Strategies for assuming agency, for learning, in tenured faculty careers. In S. Bracken, J. K. Allen, & D. R. Dean (Eds.), *The balancing act: Gendered perspectives in faculty roles and work lives* (pp. 91–120). Stylus.

O'Meara, K. (2002). Uncovering the values in faculty evaluation of service as scholarship. *Review of Higher Education, 26*(1), 57–80.

O'Meara, K. (2018, June 27). Undoing the can of worms. *Inside Higher Education*. https://www.insidehighered.com/advice/2018/06/27/how-make-faculty-service-demands-more-equitable-opinion

O'Meara, K., Kuvaeva, A., Nyunt, G., Waugaman, C., & Jackson, R. (2017). Asked more often: Gender differences in faculty workload in research universities and the work interactions that shape them. *American Educational Research Journal*, 54(6), 1154–1186.

O'Meara, K., Lounder, A., & Campbell, C. (2014). To heaven or hell: Sensemaking about why faculty leave. *Journal of Higher Education, 85*, 603–632.

O'Meara, K., Rivera, M., Kuvaeva, A., & Corrigan, K. (2017). Faculty learning matters: Organizational conditions and contexts that shape faculty learning. *Innovative Higher Education, 42*(4), 355–376.

O'Meara, K., & Terosky, A. L. (2010). Engendering faculty professional growth. *Change: The Magazine of Higher Learning, 42*(6), 44–51.

O'Meara, K., Terosky, A. L., & Neumann, A. (2008). *Faculty careers and work lives: A professional growth perspective*. ASHE Higher Education Report, 34(3). Jossey-Bass.

Oppedal, B., & Toppelberg, C. (2016). Culture competence: A developmental task of acculturation. In J. W. Berry & D. L. Sam (Eds.), *The Cambridge handbook of acculturation psychology revised* (pp. 71–92). Cambridge University Press.

Osher, D., Cantor, P., Berg, J., Steyer, L., & Rose, T. (2020). Drivers of human development: How relationships and context shape learning and development. *Applied Developmental Science, 24*(1), 6–36.

Oshin, M. (2017). *The daily routine of 20 famous writers (and how you can use them to succeed)*. Mission.org. https://medium.com/the-mission/the-daily-routine-of-20-famous-writers-and-how-you-can-use-them-to-succeed-1603f52fbb77

Pallas, A., & Neumann, A. (2019). *Convergent teaching: Tools to spark deeper learning in college*. Reforming Higher Education: Innovation and the Public Good. Johns Hopkins University Press.

Parker, K., & Lenhart, A. (2011). The digital revolution and higher education. *Pew Research Center*. http://www.pewinternet.org/2011/08/28/the-digital-revolution-and-higher-education/

Patton, L. D., & Catching, C. (2009). "Teaching while Black": Narratives of African American student affairs faculty. *International Journal of Qualitative Studies in Education, 22*(6), 713–728.

Perry, G., Moore, H., Edwards, C., Acosta, K., & Frey, C. (2009). Maintaining credibility and authority as an instructor of color in diversity-education classrooms: A qualitative inquiry. *Journal of Higher Education, 80*(1), 230–244. http://www.ohiostatepress.org/Journals/JHE/jhemain.htm.

Petrilli, L. (2012, January 25). An introvert's guide to networking. *Harvard Business Review*. https://hbr.org/2012/01/the-introverts-guide-to-networ

Philip, K., & Hendry, L. B. (2000). Making sense of mentoring or mentoring making sense? Reflections on the mentoring process by adult mentors with young people. *Journal of Community and Applied Social Psychology, 10*, 211–223.

Philipsen, M. I., & Bostic, T. B. (2010). *Helping faculty find work-life balance: The path toward family-friendly institutions*. John Wiley & Sons.

PISA: Program for Internal Student Assessment. (2003). *Student engagement at school: A sense of belonging and participation* [Survey]. Organisation for Economic Co-operation and Development.

Pittman, C. T. (2010a). Exploring how African American faculty cope with classroom racial stressors. *Journal of Negro Education*, 79, 66–78. http://gateway .proquest.com/openurl?url_ver=Z39.882004&res_dat=xri:bsc:&rft_dat=xri: bsc:ft:iibp:00389437.

Pittman, C. T. (2010b). Race and gender oppression in the classroom: The experience of women faculty of color with White male students. *Teaching Sociology*, 38(3), 183–196.

Ponjuan, L., Conley, V., & Trower, K. (2011). Career stage differences in pre-tenured track faculty perceptions of professional and personal relationships with colleagues. *Journal of Higher Education*, 82(3), 319–346.

Porter, S. R. (2007). A closer look at faculty service: What affects participation on committees? *Journal of Higher Education*, 78(5), 523–541.

Pyke, K. (2015). Faculty gender inequity and the "just say no to service" fairy tale. In K. De Welde & A. Stepnick (Eds.), *Disrupting the culture of silence* (pp. 83–95). Stylus.

Quinn, R. W. (2007). Energizing others in work relationships. In J. E. Dutton & B. R. Ragins (Eds.), *Exploring positive relationships at work: Building a theoretical and research foundation* (pp. 73–90). Routledge.

Quinn, R. W., Spreitzer, G. M., & Lam, C. F. (2012). Building a sustainable model of human energy in organizations: Exploring the critical role of resources. *Academy of Management Annals*, 6(1), 337–396.

Rhodes, C., & Fletcher, S. (2013). Coaching and mentoring for self-efficacious leadership in schools. *International Journal of Mentoring and Coaching in Education*, 2(1), 47–63. https://doi.org/10.1108/20466851311323087

Rice, R. E., & Sorcinelli, M. D. (2002). Can the tenure process be improved? In R. P. Chait (Ed.), *The questions of tenure* (pp. 101–124). Harvard University Press.

Rice, R. E., Sorcinelli, M. D., & Austin, A. E. (2000). *Heeding new voices: Academic careers for a new generation*. American Association for Higher Education.

Robbins, M. (2017). *The 5 second rule: Transform your life, work, and confidence with everyday courage*. Simon and Schuster.

Robinson, C. C., & Clardy, P. (Eds.). (2010). *Tedious journeys: Autoethnography by women of color in academe* (Vol. 375). Peter Lang.

Robison, S. (2013). *The peak performing professor: A practical guide to productivity and happiness*. John Wiley & Sons.

Rockquemore, K. A. (2015, April 8). Evaluating opportunities. *Inside Higher Ed: Career Advice*. https://www.insidehighered.com/advice/2015/m04/08/essay-how -evaluate-opportunities-may-or-may-not-help-you-win-tenure

Rockquemore, K., & Laszloffy, T. A. (2008). *The Black academic's guide to winning tenure—without losing your soul*. Lynne Rienner Publishers.

Roediger, H. L., Nestojko, J. F., & Smith, N. S. (2019). Strategies to improve learning and retention during training. In M. D. Matthews, & D. M. Schnyer, (Eds.) *Human performance optimization* (pp. 302–332). Oxford University Press.

Roeser, R. W., Midgley, C., & Urdan, T. C. (1996). Perceptions of the school psychological environment and early adolescents' psychological and behavioral functioning in school: The mediating role of goals and belonging. *Journal of Educational Psychology*, 88(3), 408–422.

Rosser, V. J. (2004). Faculty members' intentions to leave: A national study on their work life and satisfaction. *Research in Higher Education*, 45(3), 285–309.

Ryan, R. M., & Powelson, C. L. (1991). Autonomy and relatedness as fundamental to motivation and education. *Journal of Experimental Education*, 60(1), 49–66.

Salzberg, S., & Thurman, R. A. (2014). *Love your enemies: How to break the anger habit and be a whole lot happier.* Hay House Incorporated.

Scales, P. C., Benson, P. L., & Roehlkepartain, E. C. (2011). Adolescent thriving: The role of sparks, relationships, and empowerment. *Journal of Youth and Adolescence*, 40(3), 263–277.

Scott, W. R. (2013). *Institutions and organizations: Ideas, interests, and identities.* Sage Publications.

Seifert, T. A., & Umbach, P. D. (2008). The effects of faculty demographic characteristics and disciplinary context on dimensions of job satisfaction. *Research in Higher Education*, 49(4), 357–381.

Seligman, M. E. P (1991). *Learned optimism.* Knopf.

Seltzer, R. (2015). *The coach's guide for women professors: Who want a successful career and a well-balanced life.* Stylus Publishing, LLC.

Silver, M., Lochmiller, C. R., Copland, M. A., & Tripps, A. M. (2009). Supporting new school leaders: Findings from a university-based leadership coaching program for new administrators. *Mentoring & Tutoring: Partnership in Learning*, 17(3), 215–232.

Sims-Boykin, S. D., Zambrana, R. E., Williams, K. P., Salas-Lopez, D., Sheppard, V., & Headley, A. J. (2003). Mentoring underrepresented minority female medical school faculty: Momentum to increase retention and promotion. *Journal of the Association for Academic Minority Physicians*, 14(1), 15–18.

Singer, M. (2007). *The untethered soul: The journey beyond yourself.* New Harbinger Publications.

Smith, G., & Anderson, K. J. (2005). Students' ratings of professors: The teaching style contingency for Latino/a professors. *Journal of Latinos and Education*, 4(2), 115–136.

Solórzano, D. G., Allen, W. R., & Carroll, G. (2002). Keeping race in place: Racial microaggressions and campus racial climate at the University of California Berkeley. *Chicano Latino Law Review*, 23(Spring), 15–112.

Sorcinelli, M. D. (1992). New and junior faculty stress: Research and responses. *New Directions for Teaching and Learning*, 50, 27–40.

Sorcinelli, M. D., & Austin, A. E. (2006). Developing faculty for new roles and changing expectations. *Effective Practices for Academic Leaders*, 1(11), 1–16.

Sorcinelli, M. D., & Yun, J. (2007). From mentor to mentoring networks: Mentoring in the new academy. *Change: The Magazine of Higher Learning*, 39(6), 58–61.

Stack, S. (2004). Gender, children and research. *Research in Higher Education*, 45(8), 891–920.

Stanley, C. A. (2006). Coloring the academic landscape: Faculty of color breaking the silence in predominantly White colleges and universities. *American Educational Research Journal*, 43(4), 701–736.

Stanley, C. A., & Lincoln, Y. S. (2005). Cross-race faculty mentoring. *Change: The Magazine of Higher Learning*, 37(2), 44–50.

Strayhorn, T. L. (2018). *College students' sense of belonging: A key to educational success for all students*. Routledge.

Stupnisky, R. H., BrckaLorenz, A., Yuhas, B., & Guay, F. (2018). Faculty members' motivation for teaching and best practices: Testing a model based on self-determination theory across institution types. *Contemporary Educational Psychology, 53*, 15–26.

Suchman, M. C. (1995). Managing legitimacy: Strategic and institutional approaches. *Academy of Management Review, 20*(3), 571–610.

Swenson, R. (2014). *Margin: Restoring emotional, physical, financial, and time reserves to overloaded lives*. Tyndale House.

Terosky, A. L., O'Meara, K., & Campbell, C. M. (2014). Enabling possibility: Women associate professors' sense of agency in career advancement. *Journal of Diversity in Higher Education, 7*(1), 58–76. https://doi.org/10.1037/a0035775

Tierney, W., & Bensimon, E. M. (1996). *Promotion and tenure: Community and socialization in academe*. State University of New York Press.

Tolle, E. (2006). *A new earth: Awakening to your life's purpose*. Penguin Books.

Tulley, C. (2018, January 2). The importance of year 2 on the tenure track. *Inside Higher Ed*. https://www.insidehighered.com/advice/2018/01/02/second-year-make-or-break-year-gaining-tenure-opinion

Turner, C. S. V. (2002). Women of color in academe: Living with multiple marginality. *Journal of Higher Education, 73*(1), 74–93.

Turner, C. S. V., González, J. C., & Wong (Lau), K. (2011). Faculty women of color: The critical nexus of race and gender. *Journal of Diversity in Higher Education, 4*(11), 199–211.

Turner, C. S. V., González, J. C., & Wood, J. L. (2008). Faculty of color in academe: What 20 years of literature tells us. *Journal of Diversity in Higher Education, 1*(3), 139–168. https://doi.org/10.1037/a0012837

Turner, C. S. V., & Myers, S. L. (2000). *Faculty of color in academe: Bittersweet success*. Allyn & Bacon.

Twale, D. J., & Shannon, D. M. (1996). Professional service involvement of leadership faculty: An assessment of gender, role, and satisfaction. *Sex Roles, 34*(1–2), 117–126.

Uzzi, B. (2019, February 25). Research: Men and women need different kinds of networks to succeed. *Harvard Business Review*. https://hbr.org/2019/02/research-men-and-women-need-different-kinds-of-networks-to-succeed

Van Edwards, V. (2017). *Captivate: The science of succeeding with people*. Penguin.

Vargas, L. (Ed.). (2002). *Women faculty of color in the White classroom*. Peter Lang.

Villarruel, F. A., & Lerner, R. (Eds.). (1994). *Promoting community-based programs for socialization and learning*. Jossey Bass.

Wehrenberg, M. (2016, April 20). Rumination: A problem in anxiety and depression. *Psychology Today*. https://www.psychologytoday.com/us/blog/depression-management-techniques/201604/rumination-problem-in-anxiety-and-depression

Wenger, E., McDermott, R., & Snyder, W. M. (2002). *Cultivating communities of practice: A guide to managing knowledge*. Harvard University Business School Press.

Whiteside, A. L., Garrett Dikkers, A., & Lewis, S. (2014). The power of social presence for learning. *EDUCAUSE Review Online*.

Williams, S. N., Thakore, B. K., & McGee, R. (2016a). Coaching to augment mentoring to achieve faculty diversity: A randomized controlled trial. *Academic Medicine: Journal of the Association of American Medical Colleges, 91*(8), 1128–35.

Williams, S. N., Thakore, B. K., & McGee, R. (2016b). Career coaches as a source of vicarious learning for racial and ethnic minority PhD students in the biomedical sciences: A qualitative study. *PLoS one, 11*(7), e0160038. https://doi.org/10.1371/journal.pone.0160038

Wilson, R. (2012, June 3). Why are associate professors so unhappy? *Chronicle of Higher Education.* http://chronicle.com/article/Why-Are-Associate-Professors /132071/

Winslow, S. (2010). Gender inequality and time allocations among academic faculty. *Gender and Society, 24*(6), 769–793.

Zambrana, R. E., Ray, R., Espino, M. M., Castro, C., Douthirt Cohen, B., & Eliason, J. (2015). "Don't leave us behind": The importance of mentoring for underrepresented minority faculty. *American Educational Research Journal, 52*(1), 40–72.

Zerubavel, E. (1999). *The clockwork muse.* Harvard University Press.

Zuberi, T., & Bonilla-Silva, E. (Eds.). (2008). *White logic, White methods: Racism and methodology.* Rowman & Littlefield Publishers.

Index

The letter *f* after a page number refers to a figure.

ABC framework, 6*f*
Academic careers, 1, 2
Academic climate. *See* Academic culture
Academic coaching, 3, 23, 70, 78, 109
Academic code, 1, 3–4, 11–17, 23, 66–67, 109
Academic consultants. *See* Academic coaching
Academic culture, 1, 11, 13–14, 17–19, 109
Academic identity, 5–7, 48
Academic structures. *See* Academic code
Accountability structures, 94
Acosta, K., 16
Advising, 74
Age, 75
Agency
  about, 5–7
  and fulfillment, 110
  and goal setting, 83
  inner wisdom, 44–48
  and overload, 40–41
  and purpose, 2, 39–44, 49
  and self-worth, 39
Agiomavritis, J., 17, 74
Alexander-Snow, M., 68
Allen, W. R., 16–17, 20
Ambrose, S., 20, 21, 22–23
Ambrose, S. A., 22
American Council on Education, 21
Amey, M. J., 17
Anderson, K. J., 16
Andrade, H. G., 102
Antonio, A. L., 68

Assertiveness, 66, 67–68
Assessment, 101, 102, 119–120
August, L., 20, 23, 57
Austin, A. E., 3, 11, 84
Authorship issues, 62
Availability, 101

Baez, B., 61, 74
Balance. *See* Work/life balance
Bandura, A., 39
Barley, S. R., 4
Barnes, K. Y., 20
Bartlett, P. F., 3
Bauer, T. N., 11
Bavishi, A., 16
Beagan, B. L., 104
Beale, D., 32
Being present, 88
Belonging, 7, 57–58, 71–72, 74, 110
Bennett, J. C., 16, 17, 61, 74, 98, 104
Bensimon, E. M., 18, 20, 73
Benson, P. L., 57
Berg, J., 11, 57
Berglund, P., 58, 59
Bias, 1, 2, 3–5, 15–17, 23, 66–67, 103–105, 109
Bilimoria, D., 56
Bird, S., 60
Blackburn, R. T., 3, 4, 39, 73
Blanchard, K., 58
Bodner, T., 11
Body awareness, 26–27
Boice, R., 104
Bolker, J., 94
Bonilla-Silva, E., 68

Book contracts, 64
Book editors, 64
Bostic, T. B., 49, 84, 85
Boundaries, 77, 101
Bova, B., 57, 75
Bowers, E. P., 11
Boyd, T., 68
Bozeman, B., 74
Brach, T., 28
Brain and stress, 30
Brand, 50–51
BrckaLorenz, A., 5
Bresonis, K., 84
Broido, E. M., 77
Brooks, K., 104
Brown, B., 25, 30, 32, 43f, 46, 53, 56,
    89, 89f
Buchanan, C. M., 5
Burley, H., 58, 59
Butner, B. K., 58, 59

Cacioppo, J., 56
Cacioppo, J. T., 56
Cacioppo, S., 56
Cameron, T., 21
Campbell, C., 39
Campbell, C. M., 74
Cantor, P., 11, 57
Career focus, 3
Carrigan, C., 74
Carroll, G., 16–17
Castro, C., 18, 68
Catching, C., 98
Cawyer, C. S., 22
Cech, E. A., 104
Celis, S., 20, 21, 22
Cheating, 102–103
Childre, A., 86
Children, 85
Chosen service, 73–75
Cintrón, R., 68
Citing other authors, 35
Clardy, P., 68
Clark, A., 42, 43f
Clarke, M., 58
Class assignments, 102
Classroom climate, 97–98, 103–107
Classroom conflicts, 103–105

Classroom design, 106–107
Classroom equity, 103–107
COACHE (Collaborative on Academic
    Careers in Higher Education), 16,
    42–43, 60
Coaching stance, 3, 109
Codified rule of academic code, 12
Cognitive processes of institutional
    culture, 15–17
Colbeck, C., 4
Colbeck, C. L., 4, 49
Collaboration in research, 58–62
Collaborative on Academic Careers in
    Higher Education (COACHE), 16,
    42–43, 60
Collective action against grievances, 20
Collins, R., 57
Collins, S., 17
Communication styles, 66–68, 75
Communities of practice, 58, 75
Community service, 73
Community spaces, 58
Competencies and faculty development,
    7, 96
Conference participant lists, 64
Conference strategies, 62–64
Confidants, 12–13, 69
Confidence in the classroom, 97–98
Conflicts of interest, 80
Conley, V., 20
Connection. See Belonging
Connectors, 69–70
Content Sparks, 111–113
Controversial topics, 106
Copland, M. A., 3
Corrigan, K., 3, 60, 74
Costello, J., 57
Courage, 46, 53
COVID-19, 56, 85
Crenshaw, K. W., 3, 16
Csikszentmihalyi, M., 40

Daley, S., 68
Deci, E. L., 57
"Delay" strategy, 90
"Delegate" strategy, 91
"Delete" strategy, 91–92
Delgado, R., 3

Denson, N., 84
DeSouza, L., 11
Detective work, 11
Diaz, V., 73, 81
Diggs, D., 16, 17, 18, 60–61
Diggs, G. A., 18
"Diminish" strategy, 91–92
Disciplinary service, 73
Discrimination, 15–16, 18–19, 20,
    103–105
"Disputing," 27–28
Distractions from work, 93, 94
Documenting discrimination, 20
Dominant culture, 13, 57
Dominant paradigms in research,
    53–54
Dooris, M., 21
Dossiers, 21–22, 23
Double standards, 17
Douthirt Cohen, B., 18, 68
Drago, R., 4
Drennan, J., 58
Dress, 97, 98
Dunn-Rankin, P., 17
Dutton, J. E., 57
Dweck, C. S., 82

Eccles, J., 5
Edwards, C., 16
Efficiency in the classroom, 101, 102
Elder, R. W., 5
Eliason, J., 18, 68
Email handling, 91–92, 94
Energy, 40–41, 42, 78, 88, 94
Entis, L., 56
Equity, 2, 4–5, 15–17, 76, 101–102,
    109
Equity-focused service, 76
Erdogan, B., 11
Espino, M. M., 18, 68
Estrada, D., 16, 17, 18, 60–61
Ethnic norms, 67–68
Evidence of discrimination, 20
Excellence, 95
Expectations for students, 74
"Expert" in the classroom, 99
Extra income, 80
Exum, W. H., 58, 59

Faculty development, 2, 3, 5–7, 109.
    See also Recommendations for
    faculty development
Faculty diversity, 2, 17, 109
Family life, 85, 86
Fang, H., 68
Faulty collaborations, 61–62
Feedback on academic writing. See Peer
    review
Ferguson, S. K., 17
Fetridge, J. S., 17
Field-related collaborators, 60
Fixed mindset, 82
Flanagan, C., 5
Fletcher, S., 3
Flow state, 40
Ford, K. A., 16, 98
Formal tone, 97–98
Framework of this book, 3–4
Frasch, K., 84
Frey, C., 16
Friedrich, G. W., 22
Fries-Britt, S., 58, 60–61
Fritz, C., 39, 57
Fulfillment, 2, 79–80, 109–110
Furnham, A., 3

Galindo, R., 16, 17, 18, 60–61
Galinsky, E., 86
Gappa, J. M., 3
Gardner, S. K., 17
Garrett, P. B., 73, 81
Garrett Dikkers, A., 101
Garrison-Wade, D., 16, 17, 18,
    60–61
Garrison-Wade, D. F., 18
Geldhof, G. J., 11
Gender norms, 17, 56, 66, 67, 74,
    84–85
Generational divides, 75
Gestsdóttir, S., 11
Giddens, A., 4
Gillespie, K. J., 2
Gmelch, W., 22, 23
Goal setting, 83, 110, 115–118
Gonzales, L. D., 3
González, C. G., 18
González, J. C., 56, 68

Goodenow, C., 57
Gootman, J. A., 5
Goulden, M., 84, 85
Gratitude to the inner critic, 28, 30
Greene, J., 17
Grievances, 19–20
Griffin, K. A., 11, 16–17, 53, 54, 56,
        58, 59, 60–61, 68, 73, 74, 76, 98,
        104
Grover, S., 3
Growth mindset, 82
Guay, F., 5
Guest lectures, 100–101
Guida, T., 17
Guided visualization, 45–47
Guidos, M., 21
"Gut feeling," 26–27
Gutiérrez y Muhs, G., 18

Habits, 82
Hagedorn, L. S., 3
Han, J. S., 16, 20
Hanasono, L. K., 77
Hansman, C., 2
Haras, C., 3
Harm reduction, 27–28
Harris, A. P., 18
Harris, J., 16, 17, 61, 74, 98, 104
Hazelwood, A. M., 16–17, 53, 54, 58,
        59, 60, 68, 76
Headley, A. J., 68
Heaphy, E. D., 57
Hebl, M. R., 16
Hendry, L. B., 22
Herrera, T., 42
Hesli, V. L., 74
Hidden structures, 15–17
Hidden structures of institutional code,
        109. See also Academic code
Hogan, K., 3
Holmes, E., 17, 74
Howard, T. C., 16, 20
Humphrey, J. R., 16–17, 53, 54, 58,
        59, 60, 68, 76
Huston, T., 20, 21, 22–23
Huston , T. A., 22
Hyde, A., 58
Hyer, P., 21

Hypervisibility, 16
Hyun, J., 67, 70

"Identity tax," 17
Implicit bias, 15–17
Imposter syndrome, 97, 98
Inclusion, 44
Individual development, 109
Informal rules, 13–14, 66–67
Informants, 12–13
Inner critic
    about, 24–25
    body awareness, 26–27
    fixed mindset, 82
    harm reduction, 27–28
    peer review and, 32–34
    personification strategy, 27–28
    rumination, 28–30
    shame, 25–26, 32–33
    stress response, 30–31
    and teaching, 97
    writer's block, 31–32
Inner leader, 44–48
Inner wisdom, 44–48
Inspiration, 45, 79
Institutional bias, 103–105
Institutional code. See Academic code
Institutional fit, 11–12, 109–110
Institutional peers, 60
Institutional responsibility, 57
Institutional service, 73–77
Institutional structures. See Academic
        code
Instructional examples, 100
Interdisciplinary collaboration, 58–59
Interruption, 68
Isolation, 56

Jackson, R., 74
James, R., 34, 79f
Jayakumar, U., 16, 20
Job market, 2
Job satisfaction, 57
Johnsrud, L. K., 16–17
Journal editors, 63–64
Journaling, 33, 43f
Journal tiers, 52–53
Joy, S., 56

Kamler, B., 35
Kardia, D., 104
Kelly, B. T., 16, 17, 18, 58,
    60–61
Key informants, 12–13
Kimsey-House, H., 45
Kimsey-House, K., 45
Kinley, E., 73, 81
Kroth, M., 57, 75
Kulis, S., 17
Kuvaeva, A., 3, 60, 74

Ladson-Billings, G., 3–4
Lam, C. F., 39, 57, 58
Lamott, A., 31
Lander, K., 65
Laszloffy, T. A., 13, 16, 54, 56, 58, 79f,
    89, 99, 104
Lattuca, L. R., 3
Laursen, S., 17
Lawrence, C., 32
Lawrence, J. H., 3, 4, 20, 21, 22, 39, 73
Leading with your ideas, 35
Learned skills and habits, 82
Leather, P., 32
Lenhart, A., 103
Lerner, R. M., 11, 82
Lesson preparation, 99, 100
Lewis, P., 17, 54, 98
Lewis, S., 101
Li, H., 68
Li, J., 68
Liang, X., 56
Life/work balance. See Work/life
    balance
Lincoln, Y. S., 18
Link, A. N., 74
Liu, J., 68
Lochmiller, C. R., 3
Loneliness, 56
Louis, R. P., 54
Lounder, A., 39
Lundquist, J., 17, 74
Lundquist, J. H., 23, 85
Lynton, E., 73

MacIver, D., 5
Madera, J. M., 16

Maramba, D. C., 17, 18
Marbley, A. F., 58, 59
Marginalized groups.
    See Underrepresented groups
Marschke, R., 17
Martin, N. T., 15
Mason, M. A., 84, 85
Mathews, K., 43
Matoon, M., 100
Matthew, P. A., 21
McAtee, K., 2
McCann, K. I., 16, 17, 18
McDaniels, M., 11
McDermott, R., 58
McGee, R., 3, 70
McGowan, J. M., 16, 104
McKay, N. Y., 16–17
Medd, E. L., 32
Medina, E., 17
Menakem, R., 27, 31
Menges, R. J., 58, 59
Mental health, 15, 107
Mentoring, 74
Mentors, 22–23, 68–70, 75
Mertz, E. E., 20
Meyer, J. W., 13
Microaggressions, 15–16
Mid-career challenges, 42–44, 58,
    79–80
Midgley, C., 5, 57
Miller, R. A., 17
Misra, J., 17, 23, 74, 85
Mitchell, S. M., 74
Mitra, D., 5, 39
Mitra, D. L., 5, 39, 57, 58, 82
Mohamed, T., 104
Mohr, T., 26, 28, 41, 50, 67
Moore, H., 16
Moore, H. A., 16
Moore, J., 73, 81
Morgenstern, J., 82, 87, 88, 90,
    91
Motherhood, 13–14
Motivation, 57
Museus, S. D., 17, 18
Myers, S. L., 68
My Grandmother's Hands
    (Menakem), 31

Nagoski, A., 29, 88
Nagoski, E., 29, 88
Nakamura, J., 40
National School Reform Faculty
    (NSRF), 100
Negotiation, 77–78
Nestojko, J. F., 102
Networking, 62–66
Networking venues, 65–66
Neumann, A., 3, 39, 43, 44, 57, 79
New scholarship, 54–55
Nielsen, J. M., 17
Niemann, Y. F., 18
Nonassertiveness perceptions, 67–68
Nondominant groups.
    See Underrepresented groups
Nonprivileged groups.
    See Underrepresented groups
Norman, M., 20, 21, 22–23
Normative processes, 13–14, 66–67
NSRF (National School Reform
    Faculty), 100
Numbing versus recharging, 88–90
Nyunt, G., 74

Obsession with negative thoughts,
    28–30. See also Inner critic
Ombudspersons, 19
O'Meara, K., 3–4, 20, 21, 39, 57, 60,
    73, 74, 78, 81
O'Neil, D. A., 77
Online participation, 106
Online teaching, 101–102
Oppedal, B., 11
Optional service, 77–79
Osher, D., 11, 57
Oshin, M., 86
Ott, M., 20, 21, 22
Outside letter writers and
    recommenders, 70–71
Outside reviewers, 71
Overview of book, 4–7

Pacing, 98–99
Paid consulting, 80
Pallas, A., 3
Paraphrasing versus quoting, 35
Parker, K., 103

Patrick, W., 56
Patton, L. D., 98
Peak productivity times, 92–93
Peer review, 32–34, 43f
Peña, S., 77
Perfectionism, 31, 32
Perry, G., 16
Personal development, 109
Personal identity, 84
Personal values, 11
Personal web of belonging, 71–72
Personifying the inner critic, 27–28
Petrilli, L., 65
Philip, K., 22
Philipsen, M. I., 49, 84, 85
Pifer, M. J., 16–17, 53, 54, 58, 59, 60,
    68, 76
PISA (Programme for International
    Student Assessment), 57
Pittman, C. T., 16, 98, 104
Plagiarism, 102–103
Political insiders, 69
Politis, Y., 58
Ponjuan, L., 20
Pope, S. T., 86
Porter, S. R., 74
Powelson, C. L., 57
Prioritizing, 89, 90–92, 115–118
Privilege, 16, 106
Professional communities of practice, 58
Professional development benefits, 2–3
Professional service, 73
Profit ventures, 80
Programme for International Student
    Assessment (PISA), 57
Promotion and tenure. See Tenure and
    promotion
Publication strategies, 51–53
Public scholarship, 80
Publishing expectations, 51
Publishing venues, 52–53
Purpose, 11, 39–44, 50, 52, 53–54, 73,
    76, 78
Pyke, K., 3
Pyrgas, M., 32

Quality metrics, 21
Quantifying faculty evaluation, 21

Quinn, K., 74
Quinn, R. W., 57, 58

Racial bias, 56, 66
RAIN process, 28–29
Rappaport, A., 3
Ray, R., 18, 68
Recharging, 88–89
Recommendations for faculty
    development, 23, 35, 48, 55, 72,
    81, 96, 108
Recommenders, 70–71
Record keeping, 100
Reddick, R. J., 73, 74
"Relatedness," 57
Relationship building, 57, 68–70, 76
Relationships with senior faculty,
    22–23
Remote work, 85–86
Repetition of positive practices, 30
Reputation building, 63
Required service, 75–77
Research
    academic code, 3–4
    building an identity, 49–51
    challenging the status quo, 53–55
    collaborating, 16, 17, 55, 60, 74–75
    expectations for assistants, 74
    expectations of productivity, 49
    and purpose, 51–53
    as subject of classroom instruction,
        100
    values, 49–51
    visual pipeline, 86–87
Respect, 97–98
Reuman, D., 5
Rewards for productivity, 93
Reznik, V., 68
Rhodes, C., 3
Rice, R. E., 11, 20, 84
Richmond, G., 17, 98
Rigor, 95
Rincones, R., 3
Riskin, E. A., 74
Rituals and events, 13
Rivera, M., 3, 60, 74
Robbins, M., 29
Robertson, D. L., 2

Robinson, C. C., 68
Robison, S., 43f
Rockquemore, K., 13, 16, 54, 56, 58,
    79f, 89, 99, 104
Rockquemore, K. A., 53
Roediger, H. L., 102
Roehlkepartain, E. C., 57
Roeser, R. W., 5, 57
Role clarity, 11
Root, K. V., 77
Rose, T., 11, 57
Rosser, V. J., 17, 20
Rothwell, W. R., 104
Rowan, B., 13
Rubrics, 102, 119–120
Rule-following informants, 12
Rumination, 28–30
Ryan, R. M., 57

Sadao, K. C., 16–17
Sakai, K., 86
Salas-Lopez, D., 68
Salzberg, S., 42
Sandahl, P., 45
Sands, J. R., 86
Saying no, 77, 78, 79
Scales, P. C., 57
Schedule. See Time management; Time
    mapping
Schell, J., 39
Scholarly identity, 49–51
Schuh, J. H., 22, 23
Schwartz, C., 73, 81
Scott, W. R., 13, 15
Seifert, T. A., 56
Self-care, 88–90
Self-discipline, 82
Self-promotion, 50–51
Seligman, M.E.P., 27
Seltzer, R., 16, 66, 67, 68, 79f, 86, 88,
    102, 104
Serriere, S., 5, 39
Service, 60, 63, 73–80
Shame, 25–26, 32–33
Shannon, D. M., 74
Sharing your work, 50–51
Sheppard, V., 68
"Shoulds" versus "musts," 90

Sicotte, D., 17
Silver, M., 3
Simplified grading, 102–103
Simpson, R., 54
Sims-Boykin, S. D., 68
Singer, M., 25
Skills, 2, 76, 82
Smith, G., 16
Smith, N. S., 102
Smith, S., 17
Snider, J., 60–61
Snyder, W. M., 58
Social media, 50–51
Solórzano, D. G., 16–17
Sorcinelli, M. D., 11, 20, 22, 57, 84
"Soul nerve," 26–27
Sousa, B., 42, 43*f*
Speaking your truth, 34–35
Spielberger, J., 57
Sponsors, 70
Spreitzer, G. M., 39, 57, 58
Stack, S., 85
Stanley, C. A., 16–17, 18, 58, 59, 61,
    68, 74
Stefanick, J., 3
Steyer, L., 11, 57
Stockard, J., 17
Strayhorn, T. L., 57, 58
Stress response to the inner critic,
    30–31
Student assistants, 100
Student collaborations, 74, 75
Student communities of practice, 75
Student participation, 99, 101, 106–
    107
Student writing, 102
Stupnisky, R. H., 5
Suchman, M. C., 20
Support, 20–21, 59–61, 104–105, 109
Swan, C. A., 74
Swenson, R., 40
Syllabus, 98, 100, 105
Szelényi, K., 84

Task mapping, 87, 115–117
Tate, W., 3–4
Teaching
    assessment, 101, 102

being the "expert," 99
bias among students, 103–105
and boundaries, 101
classroom equity, 101–102, 103–107
classroom tone, 97–98
confidence, 97–98
controversial topics, 106
efficiency in the classroom, 101
and faculty development, 108
and guest lectures, 100–101
and the inner critic, 97
lesson preparation, 99
and marginalized groups, 104
and one's own research, 100
pacing, 98–99
record keeping, 100
respect, 97–98
student participation, 106
students assisting, 100, 106
support from senior faculty, 104–105
time management, 99
Technology use, 50–51, 89
Templer, A., 23, 85
Tenure and promotion, 16, 20–23
Teranishi, R. T., 17, 18
Terosky, A. L., 3–4, 39, 57, 74
Thakore, B. K., 3, 70
This book
    audience, 1, 109
    author's purpose, 1
    framework, 3–4
    overview, 4–7
Thomson, P., 35
Thurman, R. A., 42
Tian, M., 68
Tierney, W., 18, 20, 73
Time management, 82, 86–88, 89,
    90–92, 99, 117–118
Time mapping, 87, 88*f*, 89, 117–118
Tolbert, P. S., 4
Toles, M., 57
Tolle, E., 26
Toppelberg, C., 11
Traditional faculty development, 3
Transparency, 11
Trauma, 30–31, 46
Trice, A. G., 3
Tripps, A. M., 3

Trower, K., 20
Trust circle, 71
Truxillo, D. M., 11
Tucker, J. S., 11
Tulley, C., 23
Turner, C.S.V., 56, 68, 74
Twale, D. J., 74

Umbach, P. D., 56
Underrepresented groups, 2, 13, 16, 56,
    60–61, 68, 74, 104
University-centered faculty
    development, 3
Unwritten rules. *See* Academic code;
    Hidden structures
Urdan, T. C., 5, 57
Uzzi, B., 58, 61

Vagus nerve, 26–27
Values, 11, 42, 43*f*, 49–51, 77,
    111–113
Van Edwards, V., 65
Vargas, L., 16, 104
Villarruel, F. A., 82
Visual tools, 86–87, 115–118
Voice, 26

Wait time, 99
Waltman, J., 20, 23, 57
Waterfield, B., 104
Watkins, B., 58, 59
Waugaman, C., 74
Web of belonging, 71–72
Weekly review, 89–90
Wehrenberg, M., 29, 93
Weinberg, M., 104

Wenger, E., 58
Wharton-Michael, P., 4, 49
Wheel of Life, 83–84
Whiteside, A. L., 101
Whitworth, L., 45
Wigfield, A., 5
Wigton, T., 86
Williams, K. P., 68
Williams, S. N., 3, 70
Wilson, R., 58, 85
Wingard, D. L., 68
Winkle-Wagner, R., 60–61
Winslow, S., 74
Wong (Lau), K., 56
Wood, J. L., 68
Work conditions, 93–95, 94
Working from home, 85–86
Work/life balance, 83–86, 89,
    117–118
Work quality, 95
Work windows, 94
Wright, M., 104
Writing groups, 60
Writing habits, 31–32, 35
Wynn, J., 57

Xu, M., 68

Yacobucci, M. M., 77
Yirah, 41
Yuhas, B., 5
Yun, J., 57

Zambrana, R. E., 18, 68
Zerubavel, E., 94
Zuberi, T., 68

About the Author

Dana L. Mitra is professor of education policy studies at Pennsylvania State University. She holds a PhD from Stanford University in educational administration and policy analysis. She is founding editor of the *International Journal of Student Voice* and editor of *The American Journal of Education*. Dana also works as a leadership coach and offers coaching for faculty on writing productivity and moving through the tenure process. Dana has published extensively on the topics of student voice, civic engagement, and making a difference. She is co-author, with Stephanie C. Serriere, of *Civic Education in the Elementary Grades: Promoting Engagement in an Era of Accountability* (Teachers College Press, 2015).